THE
BOOK OF
SUCCESS

THE
BOOK OF
SUCCESS

Edited by

RICHARD SHEA

RUTLEDGE HILL PRESS
Nashville, Tennessee

Published in Nashville, Tennessee, by Rutledge Hill Press, 211 Seventh Avenue North, Nashville, Tennessee 37219. Distributed in Canada by H. B. Fenn and Company, Ltd., 1090 Lorimar Drive, Mississauga, Ontario.

Typography by D&T/Bailey, Inc., Nashville, Tennessee
Design by Bruce Gore, Gore Studios

Library of Congress Cataloging-in-Publication Data

The Book of success / edited by Richard Shea.
    p. cm.
  ISBN 1-55853-254-4
  1. Quotations, English. I. Shea, Richard, 1918– .
PN6081.B647 1993
082—dc20   93-30087
                                             CIP

Printed in the United States of America
2 3 4 5 6 7 8—98 97 96 95 94

To my good wife, Jean,
for all she has done for me.

Contents

Preface   9

1   Youth: The Best Years Of
Your Life, Or So They Say   13

2   What Will I Want To Be Doing
Every Day Ten Years From Now?   21

3   It's Almost Like Standing Aside
And Watching Yourself In Action   29

4   Is Everybody Always Trying To
Improve Themselves As I Am?   35

5   What Needs To Be Done That I Don't
Want To Do—I Must Do Today   45

6   The Quiet Power
Of Courage   51

7   How Much Money
Do I Need?   59

8   By A Lie We
Annihilate Our Dignity   67

9   You Can Win By Fraud And Deceit, But
Evil Leaves An Itch You Can't Scratch   71

10   Imagine Where We'd Be If We Didn't
Possess Our Glorious Curiosity   81

11 The Minute He Opened His Mouth
You Could Tell He Read Books   89

12 If You Take Your Time,
Thinking Is Fun   95

13 Good Health Brings You Lots Of Vigor;
And, Boy, Does That Make You Tired!   105

14 Good Talkers Go A Long
Way—Learn To Talk   111

15 A Good Laugh Is Sunshine
In The House   117

16 Let Us Swear
Eternal Friendship   121

17 Living With Nature—
Those Were The Good Times!   127

18 Happiness Is
A By-Product   141

19 And I Thought I Was The Only Person
Who Had An Inferiority Complex   149

20 The Facts
Of Life   157

21 It's The Niceties That
Make The Difference   165

22 Home: My Spot On Earth—
The Place Where I Belong   179

23 A Reminder   187

Preface

During twenty-five years as a professional speech-writer, I collected the better thoughts and observations from some of our wisest thinkers and writers. What began as an exercise to enhance my writing later turned into a habit, and then into a hobby. The result was folders full of pieces of paper all bearing exciting ideas and opinions that I considered too valuable to discard. All of these phrases had something in common. More than a conglomeration of mere words, the quotes that affected me most had contributed to my quest for success—as a professional and as a person.

In the following pages I have collected these ideas into categories that touch on all phases of successful living—career, home, money, health, pleasure, and living with nature and our fellow humans with ease and grace.

I realize there is no single formula for a happy life or for success, and that success, like happiness, is often elusive when we pursue it as an end in itself. I suspect, however, that while reading the following pages, many of you will find yourselves suddenly looking up and exclaiming, "That idea is just what I've been looking for! Perfect!"

The Book of Success is intended as a handy and regular companion. What attracted me to these quotations in the first place is the accumulated wisdom they represent. They are ideas that have guided generations on their way to enjoying rich and fulfilling lives. So refer to it often—regardless of your circumstances—for its purpose is to serve you, the reader, on your road to a successful life.

—Richard Shea

THE
BOOK OF
SUCCESS

1

Youth: The Best Years Of Your Life, Or So They Say

If one advances confidently in the direction of his dreams and endeavors to live the life he imagined, he will meet with a success unexpected in common hours.

Henry David Thoreau, American philosopher (1817–1862)

During the first period of a man's life, the danger is not to take the risk.

Sören Kierkegaard, Danish philosopher (1813–1855)

Danger and delight grow on one stalk.

Scottish proverb

Keep away from people who try to belittle your ambitions. Small people always do that, but the really great make you feel that you, too, can become great.

Mark Twain (Samuel L. Clemens), American humorist (1835–1910)

YOUTH: THE BEST YEARS OF YOUR LIFE, OR SO THEY SAY

Risk! Risk anything! Care no more for the opinion of others, for those voices. Do the hardest thing on earth for you. Act for yourself. Face the truth.

Katherine Mansfield, New Zealand-born British author (1888–1923)

If thou art a man, admire those who attempt great things, even though they fail.

Lucius Annaeus Seneca, Roman author (4 B.C.–A.D. 65)

Whatever you can do, or dream you can, begin it. Boldness has genius, power, and magic in it.

Johann Wolfgang von Goethe, German author (1749–1832)

You cannot have a proud and chivalrous spirit if your conduct is mean and paltry; for whatever a man's actions are, such must be his spirit.

Demosthenes, Greek orator (385?–322 B.C.)

Why should we be in such desperate haste to succeed, and in such desperate enterprises? If a man does not keep pace with his companions, perhaps it is because he hears a different drummer. Let him step to the music which he hears, however measured and far away. It is not important that he should mature as soon as an apple tree or an oak.

Henry David Thoreau, American philosopher (1817–1862)

There is the greatest practical benefit in making a few failures early in life.

Thomas Henry Huxley, British zoologist (1825–1895)

Youth is the time to go flashing from one end of the world to the other . . . to try the manners of different nations; to hear the chimes at midnight; to see the sunrise in town and country; to be converted at a revival; to circumnavigate the metaphysics, write halting verses, run a mile to see a fire, and wait all day long in the theatre to applaud *Hernani*.

Robert Louis Stevenson, Scottish author (1850–1894)

YOUTH: THE BEST YEARS OF YOUR LIFE, OR SO THEY SAY

And above all things, never think that you're not good enough yourself. A man should never think that. My belief is that in life people will take you at your own reckoning.

Anthony Trollope, British author (1815–1882)

It is a great art to saunter.

Henry David Thoreau, American philosopher (1817–1862)

The supreme end of education is expert discernment in all things—the power to tell the good from the bad, the genuine from the counterfeit, and to prefer the good and the genuine to the bad and the counterfeit.

Samuel Johnson, British author and lexicographer (1709–1784)

Only two kids enjoy high school. One is captain of the football team, and the other is his girl friend.

Letter to Ann Landers

YOUTH: THE BEST YEARS OF YOUR LIFE, OR SO THEY SAY

In my last two years in high school, my face was pocked with pimples, I stammered when I spoke; if I made a mistake, I blushed furiously, and when nervous, as I was in the company of girls, I perspired freely.

Joseph L————, successful trial lawyer

Whom do I call educated? First, those who manage well the circumstances they encounter day by day. . . . Next, those who are decent and honorable in their intercourse with all men, bearing easily and good naturedly what is offensive in others and being as agreeable and reasonable to their associates as is humanly possible to be . . . those who hold their pleasures always under control and are not ultimately overcome by their misfortunes . . . those who are not spoiled by their successes, who do not desert their true selves but hold their ground steadfastly as wise and sober-minded men.

Socrates, Greek philosopher (470?–399 B.C.)

It is almost the definition of a gentleman to say that he is one who never inflicts pain.

Cardinal John Henry Newman, British prelate and theologian (1801–1890)

Grace is the absence of everything that indicates pain or difficulty, hesitation or incongruity.

William Hazlitt, British essayist (1778–1830)

Politeness is to human nature what warmth is to wax.

Arthur Schopenhauer, German philosopher (1788–1860)

My candle burns at both ends;
It will not last the night;
But, ah, my foes, and, oh, my friends—
It gives a lovely light.

Edna St. Vincent Millay, American poet (1892–1950)

On with the dance! Let joy be unconfined;
No sleep till morn when Youth and Pleasure meet
To chase the glowing Hours with flying feet.

*George Gordon, Lord Byron, British poet
(1788–1824)*

She knew how to trust people . . . a rare
quality, revealing a character far above average.

*Cardinal Jean François de Retz, French politician
and man of letters (1614–1679)*

 Courage and perseverance have a magical
talisman, before which difficulties disappear and
obstacles vanish into air.

John Quincy Adams, U.S. president (1767–1848)

There is no accounting for tastes, as the
woman said when someone told her her son was
wanted by the police.

*Franklin Pierce Adams (F. P. A.), American
journalist (1881–1960)*

YOUTH: THE BEST YEARS OF YOUR LIFE, OR SO THEY SAY

2

What Will
I Want To Be
Doing Every
Day Ten Years
From Now?

It is the first of all problems for a man to find out what kind of work he is to do in this universe.

Thomas Carlyle, Scottish author (1795–1881)

I am a writer because writing is the thing I do best.

Flannery O'Connor, American author (1925–1964)

The world judge of men by their ability in their professions, and we judge of ourselves by the same test; for it is on that on which our success in life depends.

William Hazlitt, British essayist (1778–1830)

The man who is born with a talent which he was meant to use finds his greatest happiness in using it.

Johann Wolfgang von Goethe, German author (1749–1832)

WHAT WILL I WANT TO BE DOING EVERY DAY TEN YEARS FROM NOW?

The test of a vocation is the love of the drudgery it involves.

Logan Pearsall Smith, American essayist (1865–1946)

Anything you're good at contributes to happiness.

Bertrand Russell, British philosopher (1872–1970)

When work is a pleasure, life is a joy! When work is duty, life is slavery.

Maxim Gorky, Russian author (1868–1936)

We could hardly wait to get up in the morning!

Wilbur Wright and Orville Wright, American inventors (1867–1912; 1871–1948)

What is work and what is not work are questions that perplex the wisest of men.

The Bhagavad-Gita, *Hindu holy book*

WHAT WILL I WANT TO BE DOING EVERY DAY
TEN YEARS FROM NOW?

I go on working for the same reason that a hen goes on laying eggs. There is in every living creature an obscure but powerful impulse to active functioning. Life demands to be lived. Inaction, save as a measure of recuperation between bursts of activity, is painful and dangerous to the healthy organism—in fact, it is almost impossible. Only the dying can be really idle.

Henry Louis (H. L.) Mencken, American author (1880–1956)

 If people only knew how hard I work to gain my mastery, it wouldn't seem so wonderful at all.

Michelangelo Buonarroti, Italian artist (1475–1564)

 I never did anything worth doing by accident; nor did any of my inventions come by accident; they came by work.

Thomas Alva Edison, American inventor (1847–1931)

WHAT WILL I WANT TO BE DOING EVERY DAY
TEN YEARS FROM NOW?

Leisure may be defined as free activity, labor as compulsory activity. Leisure does what it likes, labor does what it must, the compulsion being that of Nature, which in these latitudes leaves men no choice between labor and starvation.

George Bernard Shaw, Irish-born British playwright (1856–1950)

If he [Tom Sawyer] had been a great and wise philosopher, like the writer of this book, he would now have comprehended that Work consists of whatever a body is *obliged* to do and Play consists of whatever a body is not obliged to do.

Mark Twain (Samuel L. Clemens), American humorist (1835–1910)

Labor is the curse of the world, and nobody can meddle with it without becoming proportionately brutified.

Nathaniel Hawthorne, American author (1804–1864)

WHAT WILL I WANT TO BE DOING EVERY DAY
TEN YEARS FROM NOW?

Inspiration comes of working every day.

Charles Pierre Baudelaire, French poet
(1821–1867)

Infatuated, half through conceit, half through love of my art, I achieve the impossible working as no one else ever works.

Alexandre Dumas, French author (1824–1895)

Lord, grant that I may always desire more than I can accomplish.

Michelangelo Buonarroti, Italian artist (1475–1564)

Whatsoever thy hand findeth to do, do it with thy might; for there is no work, or device, nor knowledge, nor wisdom, in the grave whither thou goest.

Ecclesiastes

WHAT WILL I WANT TO BE DOING EVERY DAY
TEN YEARS FROM NOW?

They talk of the dignity of work. The dignity is in leisure.

Herman Melville, American author (1819–1891)

Let us do our duty in our shop or in our kitchen, in the market, the street, the office, the school, the home, just as faithfully as if we stood in the front rank of some great battle, and knew that victory for mankind depends on our bravery, strength, and skill. When we do that, the humblest of us will be serving in that great army which achieves the welfare of the world.

Theodore Parker, American clergyman (1810–1860)

One chops the wood, the other does the grunting.

Yiddish proverb

Anything for the quiet life, as the man said when he took the situation at the lighthouse.

Charles Dickens, British author (1812–1870)

WHAT WILL I WANT TO BE DOING EVERY DAY
TEN YEARS FROM NOW?

A man is a worker. If he is not, then he is nothing.

Joseph Conrad, Polish-born British author (1857–1924)

The precise form of an individual's activity is determined, of course, by the equipment with which he came into the world. In other words, it is determined by his heredity.

Henry Louis (H. L.) Mencken, American author (1880–1956)

3

It's Almost
Like Standing
Aside And
Watching Yourself
In Action

Who in the world am I? Ah, that's the great puzzle.

Lewis Carroll (Charles L. Dodgson), British mathematician and author (1832–1898)

Know thyself.

Delphi temple inscription

One must know oneself. If this does not serve to discover truth, it at least serves as a rule of life and there is nothing better.

Blaise Pascal, French philosopher and mathematician (1623–1662)

People seem not to see that their opinion of the world is also a confession of character.

Ralph Waldo Emerson, American author (1803–1882)

A man generally has the good or ill qualities he attributes to mankind.

William Shenstone, British poet (1714–1763)

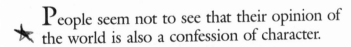

IT'S ALMOST LIKE STANDING ASIDE AND WATCHING
YOURSELF IN ACTION

Few men are of one plain, decided color; most are mixed, shaded or blended; and vary as much from different situations, as changeable silks do from different lights.

Philip Dormer Stanhope, Earl of Chesterfield, English statesman and author (1694–1773)

I have often thought the best way to define a man's character would be to seek out the particular mental or moral attitude in which, when it came upon him, he felt himself most deeply and intensely active and alive. At such moments there is a voice inside which speaks and says: "This is the real me!"

William James, American psychologist and philosopher (1842–1910)

The world is a looking glass, and gives back to every man the reflection of his own face.

William Makepeace Thackeray, British author (1811–1863)

IT'S ALMOST LIKE STANDING ASIDE AND WATCHING YOURSELF IN ACTION

It is with trifles and when he is off guard that a man best reveals his character.

Arthur Schopenhauer, German philosopher
(1788–1860)

 What you do speaks so loud that I cannot hear what you say.

Ralph Waldo Emerson, American author
(1803–1882)

I know myself as a human entity; the scene, so to speak, of thoughts and affections; and am sensible of certain doubleness by which I can stand as remote from myself as from another. However intense my experience, I am conscious of the presence and criticism of a part of me, which, as it were, is not part of me, but spectator, sharing no experience, but taking note of it, and that is no more I than it is you.

Henry David Thoreau, American philosopher
(1817–1862)

IT'S ALMOST LIKE STANDING ASIDE AND WATCHING
YOURSELF IN ACTION

At bottom every man knows well enough that he is a unique being, only once on this earth; and by no extraordinary chance will such a marvelously picturesque piece of diversity in unity as he is, ever be put together a second time.

Friedrich Wilhelm Nietzsche, German philosopher (1844–1900)

Know thyself. A maxim as pernicious as it is ugly. Whoever studies himself arrests his own development. A caterpillar who seeks to know himself would never become a butterfly.

André Gide, French author (1869–1951)

Our works are the mirror wherein the spirit first sees its natural lineaments. Hence, too, the folly of that impossible precept, Know thyself; till it be translated into this partially possible one, Know what thou canst work at.

Thomas Carlyle, Scottish author (1795–1881)

IT'S ALMOST LIKE STANDING ASIDE AND WATCHING YOURSELF IN ACTION

A man never describes his own character so clearly as when he describes another.

Jean Paul Richter, German satirist (1763–1825)

I want, by understanding myself, to understand others. I want to be all that I am capable of becoming. . . . This all sounds very strenuous and serious. But now that I have wrestled with it, it's no longer so. I feel happy—deep down. All is well.

Katherine Mansfield, New Zealand-born British author (1888–1923)

It was prettily devised of Aesop, "The fly sat on the axle tree of the chariot wheel and said, 'What dust do I raise!'"

Francis Bacon, English statesman, philosopher, and essayist (1561–1626)

Is
Everybody
Always Trying To
Improve Themselves
As I Am?

To live is to change, and to be perfect is to have changed often.

Cardinal John Henry Newman, British prelate and theologian (1801–1890)

For who is pleased with himself?

Samuel Johnson, British author and lexicographer (1709–1784)

Who is not satisfied with himself will grow; who is not so sure of his own correctness will learn many things.

Palestinian maxim

Men acquire a particular quality by constantly acting a particular way. . . . We become just by performing just actions, temperate by performing temperate actions, brave by performing brave actions.

Aristotle, Greek philosopher (384–322 B.C.)

IS EVERYBODY ALWAYS TRYING
TO IMPROVE THEMSELVES AS I AM?

He who asks of life nothing but the improvement of his own nature . . . is less liable than anyone else to miss and waste life.

General Henri Frédéric Amiel, Swiss educator and philosopher (1821–1881)

I tell you that as long as I can conceive something better than myself I cannot be easy unless I am striving to bring it into existence or clearing the way for it.

George Bernard Shaw, Irish-born British playwright (1856–1950)

Human beings, by changing the inner attitudes of their minds, can change the outer aspects of their lives.

William James, American psychologist and philosopher (1842–1910)

We must always change, renew, rejuvenate ourselves; otherwise we harden.

Johann Wolfgang von Goethe, German author (1749–1832)

IS EVERYBODY ALWAYS TRYING
TO IMPROVE THEMSELVES AS I AM?

The duty of man is the same in respect to his own nature as in respect to the nature of all other things, namely not to follow it but to amend it.

John Stuart Mill, British economist and philosopher (1806–1873)

How could there be any question of acquiring or possessing, when the one thing needful for a man is to become—to be at last, and to die in the fullness of his being.

Antoine de Saint-Exupéry, French aviator and author (1900–1944)

 It is necessary to try to surpass one's self always; this occupation ought to last as long as life.

Christina, Swedish queen (1626–1689)

 I realized the problem was me and nobody could change me except myself.

John Petworth, British essayist (1835–1904)

IS EVERYBODY ALWAYS TRYING
TO IMPROVE THEMSELVES AS I AM?

There is nothing that can be changed more completely than human nature when the job is taken in hand early enough.

George Bernard Shaw, Irish-born British playwright (1856–1950)

The never-ending task of self improvement . . .

Ralph Waldo Emerson, American author (1803–1882)

The hell to be endured hereafter, of which theology tells, is no worse than the hell we make for ourselves in this world by habitually fashioning our characters in the wrong way.

William James, American psychologist and philosopher (1842–1910)

Every action we take, everything we do, is either a victory or defeat in the struggle to become what we want to be.

Anne Byrhhe, Norwegian family counselor (1906–1981)

IS EVERYBODY ALWAYS TRYING
TO IMPROVE THEMSELVES AS I AM?

I have discovered that we may be in some degree whatever character we choose. Besides, practice forms a man to anything.

James Boswell, Scottish biographer (1740–1795)

The self is not something ready-made, but something in continuous formation through choice of action.

John Dewey, American educator and philosopher (1859–1952)

It is enough that we set out to mold the motley stuff of life into some form of our own choosing; when we do, the performance is itself the wage.

Learned Hand, American jurist (1872–1961)

I know of no more encouraging fact than the unquestioned ability of a man to elevate his life by conscious endeavor.

Henry David Thoreau, American philosopher (1817–1862)

IS EVERYBODY ALWAYS TRYING
TO IMPROVE THEMSELVES AS I AM?

There is a form of eminence which does not depend on fate; it is an air which sets us apart and seems to portend great things; it is the value which we unconsciously attach to ourselves; it is the quality which wins us deference of others; more than birth, position, or ability, it gives us ascendance.

François, Duc de La Rochefoucauld, French author (1613–1680)

Habit, if not resisted, soon becomes necessity. ✦

Saint Augustine, North African-born church father (354–430)

We must make automatic and habitual, as early as possible, as many useful actions as we can . . . in the acquisition of a new habit, we must take care to launch ourselves with as strong and decided initiative as possible. . . . Never suffer an exception to occur till the new habit is securely rooted in your life.

William James, American psychologist and philosopher (1842–1910)

IS EVERYBODY ALWAYS TRYING
TO IMPROVE THEMSELVES AS I AM?

We sow our thoughts, and we reap our actions.
We sow our actions, and we reap our habits.
We sow our habits, and we reap our characters;
We sow our characters, and we reap our destiny.

Anonymous

Character is simply habit long continued.

Plutarch, Greek biographer and philosopher (46?–120?)

Long years must pass before the truths we have made for ourselves become our very flesh.

Paul Ambroise Valéry, French poet (1871–1945)

The creation of Cary Grant took more than the accent; it took time and practice on the walk, the talk, and all those other mannerisms. "I pretended to be somebody I wanted to be, and I finally became that person," Mr. Grant said, "or he became me. Or we met at some point. It's a relationship."

Washington Post *obituary of actor Cary Grant*

IS EVERYBODY ALWAYS TRYING
TO IMPROVE THEMSELVES AS I AM?

I am often confronted by the necessity of standing by one of my empirical selves and relinquishing the rest. Not that I would not, if I could, be . . . a great athlete and make a million a year, be a wit, a bon-vivant and a lady killer, as well as a philosopher, a philanthropist . . . and saint. But the thing is simply impossible. The millionaire's work would run counter to the saint's; the bon-vivant and the philanthropist would trip each other up; the philosopher and the lady killer could not well keep house in the same tenement of clay. Such different characters may conceivably, at the outset of life, be alike possible for a man. But to make any one of them actual, the rest must more or less be suppressed. So the seeker of his truest, strongest, deepest self must review the list carefully and pick out one on which to stake his salvation. All other selves thereupon become unreal, but the fortunes of this self are real. Its failures are real failures, its triumphs real triumphs carrying shame and gladness with them.

William James, American psychologist and philosopher (1842–1910)

IS EVERYBODY ALWAYS TRYING
TO IMPROVE THEMSELVES AS I AM?

How use doth breed a habit in man!

William Shakespeare, English dramatist
(1564–1616)

Withdraw into yourself and look. And if you do not find yourself beautiful yet, act as does the creator of a statue that is to be made beautiful: he cuts away here, he smoothes there, he makes this line lighter, this other purer, until a lovely face has grown upon his work. So do you also: cut away all that is excessive, straighten all that is crooked, bring light to all that is overcast, labor to make all one glow of beauty and never cease chiseling your statue, until there shall shine out on you from it the godlike splendor of virtue, until you see the perfect goodness surely established in the stainless shrine.

Plotinus, Egyptian-born Roman philosopher
(205?–270)

IS EVERYBODY ALWAYS TRYING
TO IMPROVE THEMSELVES AS I AM?

5

What Needs To Be Done That I Don't Want To Do—I Must Do Today

We distinguish the excellent man from the common man by saying that the former is the one who makes great demands on himself, and the latter who makes no demands on himself.

José Ortega y Gasset, Spanish philosopher, author, and politician (1883–1955)

I have known many who could not when they would, for they had not done it when they could.

François Rabelais, French author (1494?–1553)

To will is to select a goal, determine a course of action that will bring one to that goal, and then hold to that action till the goal is reached. The key is action.

Michael Hanson, American mathematician (1863–1908)

You must do the thing you think you cannot do.

Eleanor Roosevelt, American diplomat, author, First Lady (1884–1962)

WHAT NEEDS TO BE DONE THAT I DON'T WANT TO DO—
I MUST DO TODAY

Whether you find satisfaction in life depends not on your tale of years, but on your will.

Michel Eyquem de Montaigne, French essayist (1533–1592)

They can because they think they can.

Virgil (Publius Vergilius Maro), Roman poet (70–19 B.C.)

The will of a man is his happiness.

Johann Christoph Friedrich von Schiller, German poet, playwright, and historian (1759–1805)

A man can do all things if he but wills them.

Leon Battista Alberti, Italian architect (1404–1472)

As the Sandwich Islander believes that the strength and valor of the enemy he kills passes into himself, so we gain the strength of the temptation we resist.

Ralph Waldo Emerson, American author (1803–1882)

WHAT NEEDS TO BE DONE THAT I DON'T WANT TO DO—
I MUST DO TODAY

We improve ourselves by victories over ourself. There must be contests, and we must win.

Edward Gibbon, British historian (1737–1794)

Deny yourself! You must deny yourself! That is the song that never ends.

Johann Wolfgang von Goethe, German author (1749–1832)

It is energy—the central element of which is will—that produces the miracle that is enthusiasm in all ages. Everywhere it is what is called force of character and the sustaining power of all great action.

Samuel Smiles, Scottish author (1812–1904)

Cheerfulness in most cheerful people is the rich and satisfying result of strenuous discipline.

Edwin Percy Whipple, American essayist (1819–1886)

WHAT NEEDS TO BE DONE THAT I DON'T WANT TO DO—
I MUST DO TODAY

Perhaps the most valuable result of all education is the ability to make yourself do the thing you have to do, when it ought to be done, whether you like it or not; it is the first lesson that ought to be learned; and however early a man's training begins, it is probably the last lesson he learns thoroughly.

Thomas Henry Huxley, British zoologist (1825–1895)

Do every day or two something for no other reason than you would rather not do it, so that when the hour of dire need draws nigh, it may find you not unnerved and untrained to stand the test.

William James, American psychologist and philosopher (1842–1910)

Most powerful is he who has himself in his own power.

Lucius Annaeus Seneca, Roman author (4 B.C.–A.D. 65)

WHAT NEEDS TO BE DONE THAT I DON'T WANT TO DO— I MUST DO TODAY

The undertaking of a new action brings new strength.

Evenius, Roman writer (42 B.C.–A.D. 13)

We never know how high we are
Till we are called to rise.
And then, if we are true to plan,
Our statures touch the skies.

Emily Dickinson, American poet (1830–1886)

Never give in,
never give in
never, never, never, never
in nothing great or small,
large or petty—
never give in.

Winston Churchill, British statesman (1874–1965)

 Who then is free? The wise man who can govern himself.

Horace (Quintus Horatius Flaccus), Roman poet (65–8 B.C.)

WHAT NEEDS TO BE DONE THAT I DON'T WANT TO DO—
I MUST DO TODAY

The Quiet Power Of Courage

If we take the generally accepted definition of bravery as a quality which knows no fear, I have never seen a brave man. All men are frightened. The more intelligent they are, the more they are frightened.

General George S. Patton, American general (1885–1945)

I believe that anyone can conquer fear by doing the things he fears to do, provided he keeps doing them until he gets a record of successful experiences behind him.

Eleanor Roosevelt, American diplomat, author, First Lady (1884–1962)

The bravest thing you can do when you are not brave is to profess courage and act accordingly.

Corra Harris, American writer (1869–1935)

Be still my heart; thou hast known worse than this.

Homer, Greek poet (c. 850? B.C.)

Let a man who has to make his fortune in life remember this maxim: Attacking is the only secret. Dare and the world yields, or if it beats you sometimes, dare it again and it will succeed.

William Makepeace Thackeray, British author
(1811–1863)

Go on and increase in valor, O Boy, this is the path to immortality.

Virgil (Publius Vergilius Maro), Roman poet
(70–19 B.C.)

Facing it, always facing it, that's the way to get through. Face it.

Joseph Conrad, Polish-born British author
(1857–1924)

I would define true courage to be a perfect sensibility of the measure of danger, and a mental willingness to endure it.

General William Tecumseh Sherman, American
Union general (1820–1891)

A light supper, a good night's sleep, and a fine morning have sometimes made a hero of the same man who, by an indigestion, a restless night, and a rainy morning would have proved a coward.

Philip Dormer Stanhope, Earl of Chesterfield, English statesman and author (1694–1773)

You have endured worse things; God will grant an end even to these.

Virgil (Publius Vergilius Maro), Roman poet (70–19 B.C.)

Courage stands halfway between cowardice and rashness, one of which is a lack, the other an excess of courage.

Plutarch, Greek biographer and philosopher (46?–120?)

Death was afraid of him because he had the heart of a lion.

Arab proverb

Courage is doing what you're afraid to do. There can be no courage unless you are scared.

Edward Vernon (Eddie) Rickenbacker, American aviator and businessman (1890–1973)

Take calculated risks. That is quite different from being rash.

General George S. Patton, American general (1885–1945)

The desire for safety stands against every great and noble enterprise.

Publius Cornelius Tacitus, Roman historian and orator (55?–120?)

You gain strength, courage, and confidence by each experience in which you really stop to look fear in the face. You are able to say to yourself, "I have lived through this horror. I can take the next thing that comes along."

Eleanor Roosevelt, American diplomat, author, First Lady (1884–1962)

Courage is the price life exacts for granting peace.

Amelia Earhart, American aviator (1897–1937?)

What a new face courage puts on everything!

Ralph Waldo Emerson, American author (1803–1882)

Believe me! The secret of reaping the greatest fruitfulness and the greatest enjoyment from life is to live dangerously!

Friedrich Wilhelm Nietzsche, German philosopher (1844–1900)

Prudence operates on life in the same manner as rules of composition; it produces vigilance rather than elevation; rather prevents loss than procures advantage; and often miscarriages, but seldom reaches either power or honor.

Samuel Johnson, British author and lexicographer (1709–1784)

I must tell you I take terrible risks. Because my playing is very clear, when I make a mistake you hear it. If you want me to play only the notes without any specific dynamics, I will never make one mistake. Never be afraid to dare.

Vladimir Horowitz, Russian-born American pianist (1904–1989)

Shun security.

Thales of Miletos, Greek philosopher and mathematician (640?–546 B.C.)

I am ready any time. Do not keep me waiting.

John Brown, American abolitionist (1800–1859), on the scaffold

Play the man, Master Ridley; we shall this day light such a candle, by God's grace in England, as I trust shall never be put out.

Hugh Latimer, English prelate and religious reformer (1485–1555) to his colleague, Nicholas Ridley, while being burned at the stake for heresy, Oxford, October 16, 1555

THE QUIET POWER OF COURAGE

What doesn't kill me only makes me stronger.

Friedrich Wilhelm Nietzsche, German philosopher
(1844–1900)

I went out to Charing Cross to see Major
General Harrison hanged, drawn, and
quartered; which was done there, he looking as
cheerful as any man could in that condition.

Samuel Pepys, English diarist (1633–1703)

On his mounting the scaffold to be beheaded:
"I pray you, Master Lieutenant, see me safely
up, and for my coming down, let me shift for
myself."

To the executioner: "Pick up thy spirits, Man,
and be not afraid to do thyne office; my neck is
very short; take heed, therefore thou strike not
awry, for saving of thyne honesty."

Saint (Sir) Thomas More, English statesman and
author (1478–1535)

How
Much
Money Do
I Need?

The only thing I like about rich people is their money.

Nancy, Lady Astor, American-born British politician
(1879–1964)

Money is the most important thing in the world. It represents health, strength, honor, generosity, and beauty as conspicuously as the want of it represents illness, weakness, disgrace, meanness, and ugliness.

George Bernard Shaw, Irish-born British playwright
(1856–1950)

Ready money is Aladdin's lamp.

George Gordon, Lord Byron, British poet
(1788–1824)

There are few sorrows, however poignant, in which a good income is to no avail.

Logan Pearsall Smith, American essayist
(1865–1947)

HOW MUCH MONEY DO I NEED?

I cannot afford to waste my time making money.

Louis Agassiz, Swiss-born American naturalist (1807–1873)

But it is a pretty thing to see what money will do!

Samuel Pepys, English diarist (1633–1703)

Many a man has found the acquisition of wealth only a change, not an end, of miseries.

Lucius Annaeus Seneca, Roman author (4 B.C.–A.D. 65)

The most valuable of all human possessions, next to a superior and disdainful air, is the reputation of being well-to-do.

Henry Louis (H. L.) Mencken, American author (1880–1956)

Every increased possession loads us with a new weariness.

John Ruskin, British author and critic (1819–1900)

I think I could be a good woman if I had five thousand a year.

Becky Sharp, character in the novel Vanity Fair, *by William Makepeace Thackeray, British author (1811–1863)*

Riches are chiefly good because they give us time.

Charles Lamb, British essayist (1775–1834)

The day, water, sun, moon, night—I do not have to purchase these things with money.

Titus Maccius Plautus, Roman playwright (254?–184 B.C.)

A large income is the best recipe for happiness I ever heard of.

Jane Austen, British author (1775–1817)

HOW MUCH MONEY DO I NEED?

So our Lord God commonly gave riches to those gross asses to whom he vouchsafed nothing else.

Martin Luther, German Protestant religious reformer (1483–1546)

Does he counsel you better who bids you, "Money, by right means, if you can; but by any means, make money"?

Horace (Quintus Horatius Flaccus), Roman poet (65–8 B.C.)

It is easier for a camel to pass through the eye of the needle than for a rich man to enter the Kingdom of God.

Jesus of Nazareth

All heiresses are beautiful.

John Dryden, English author (1631–1700)

He who marries for money earns it.

Yiddish proverb

HOW MUCH MONEY DO I NEED?

How many are the things I can do without!

Socrates, Greek philosopher (470?–399 B.C.)

The love of money grows as the money itself grows.

Juvenal (Decimus Junius Juvenalis), Roman satirist (60?–140?)

With the great part of rich people, the chief employment of riches consists in the parade of riches.

Adam Smith, Scottish political economist and philosopher (1723–1790)

What's the point of having money if nobody knows it!

Well-dressed woman in a Cadillac showroom

Don't spend your money till you have it.

Thomas Jefferson, U.S. president (1743–1826)

HOW MUCH MONEY DO I NEED?

Nowadays nothing but money counts: a fortune brings honors, friendships, the poor man everywhere lies low.

Ovid (Publius Ovidius Naso), Roman poet (43 B.C.–A.D. 18)

We read on the foreheads of those who are surrounded by a foolish luxury, that Fortune sells what she is thought to give.

Jean de La Fontaine, French poet and fabulist (1621–1695)

In order to stand well in the eyes of the community, it is necessary to come up to a certain, somewhat indefinite, conventional standard of wealth.

Thorsten Veblen, American economist (1857–1929)

After spending some money in his sleep, Hermon the Miser was so infuriated that he hanged himself.

Gaius Lucilius, Roman satirist (180–103? B.C.)

HOW MUCH MONEY DO I NEED?

What do we call love, hate, charity, revenge, humanity, forgiveness? Different results of the master impulse, the necessity of securing one's self-approval.

Mark Twain (Samuel L. Clemens), American humorist (1835–1910)

Others have done it before me. I can, too.

Corporal John Faunce, letter to his family, World War II

CHAPTER

8

By A
Lie We
Annihilate
Our Dignity

One may sometimes tell a lie, but the grimace that accompanies it tells the truth.

Friedrich Wilhelm Nietzsche, German philosopher (1844–1900)

In plain truth, lying is an accursed vice. We are not men, nor have any other tie upon another, but by our word.

Michel Eyquem de Montaigne, French essayist (1533–1592)

I detest the man who hides one thing in the depth of his heart and speaks forth another.

Homer, Greek poet (c. 850? B.C.)

Society can exist only on the basis that there is some amount of polished lying and that no one says exactly as he thinks.

Lin Yutang, Chinese-born American philologist (1895–1976)

BY A LIE WE ANNIHILATE OUR DIGNITY

I do myself a greater injury in lying than I do him of whom I tell a lie.

Michel Eyquem de Montaigne, French essayist (1533–1592)

Nobody speaks the truth when there's something they must have.

Elizabeth Bowen, Irish-born British author (1899–1973)

By a lie, a man . . . annihilates his dignity as a man.

Immanuel Kant, German philosopher (1724–1804)

Lies are essential to humanity. They are perhaps as important as the pursuit of pleasure and moreover are dictated by that pursuit.

Marcel Proust, French author (1871–1922)

The foundation of morality is to have done, once and for all, with lying.

Thomas Henry Huxley, British zoologist (1825–1895)

I speak truth, not as much as I would, but as much as I dare; and I dare a little the more as I grow older.

Michel Eyquem de Montaigne, French essayist (1533–1592)

He was the consummate politician. He didn't lie, neither did he tell the truth.

John Lundberg, American political writer (1885–1962)

Lying is not only excusable; it is not only innocent; it is, above all, necessary and unavoidable. Without the ameliorations that it offers, life would become a mere syllogism and hence too metallic to be borne.

Henry Louis (H. L.) Mencken, American author (1880–1956)

 A half truth is a whole lie.

Yiddish proverb

You Can Win By Fraud And Deceit, But Evil Leaves An Itch You Can't Scratch

There is one thing alone that stands the brunt of life throughout its length: a quiet conscience.

Euripides, Greek dramatist (480?–406 B.C.)

What doth it profit a man if he gains the whole world and loses his own soul?

Jesus of Nazareth

And if your friend does evil to you, say to him, "I forgive you for what you did to me, but how can I forgive you for what you did to yourself?"

Friedrich Wilhelm Nietzsche, German philosopher (1844–1900)

Only a life lived in the service to others is worth living.

Albert Einstein, German-born American physicist (1879–1955)

Honesty is for the most part less profitable than dishonesty.

Plato, Greek philosopher (427?–347 B.C.)

YOU CAN WIN BY FRAUD AND DECEIT,
BUT EVIL LEAVES AN ITCH YOU CAN'T SCRATCH

Among the attributes of God, although they are all equal, mercy shines with even more brilliance than justice.

Miguel de Cervantes Saavadra, Spanish author (1547–1616)

With all humility, I think, "Whatsoever thy hand findeth to do, do it with thy might" infinitely more important than the vain attempt to love one's neighbor as one's self. If you want to hit a bird on the wing, you must have all your will in focus, you must not be thinking about yourself, and equally, you must not be thinking about your neighbor: you must be living in your eye on that bird. Every achievement is a bird on the wing.

Oliver Wendell Holmes, Jr., American jurist (1841–1935)

When I do good, I feel good. When I do bad, I feel bad. And that's my religion.

Abraham Lincoln, U.S. president (1809–1865)

YOU CAN WIN BY FRAUD AND DECEIT,
BUT EVIL LEAVES AN ITCH YOU CAN'T SCRATCH

There is a set of religious, or rather moral, writings which teach that virtue is the certain road to happiness, and vice to misery in this world. A very wholesome and comfortable doctrine, and to which we have but one objection, namely, that it is not true.

Henry Fielding, British author (1707–1754)

Life is unfair.

John F. Kennedy, U.S. president (1917–1963)

As for doing good; that is one of the professions which is full. Moreover I have tried it fairly and, strange as it may seem, am satisfied that it does not agree with my constitution.

Henry David Thoreau, American philosopher (1817–1862)

 Do unto others as you would have them do unto you.

Jesus of Nazareth

YOU CAN WIN BY FRAUD AND DECEIT,
BUT EVIL LEAVES AN ITCH YOU CAN'T SCRATCH

The rule of joy and the law of duty seem to me all one.

Oliver Wendell Holmes, Jr., American jurist (1841–1935)

The ideals that have lighted my way and, time after time, have given me new courage to face life cheerfully have been Kindness, Beauty, and Truth.

Albert Einstein, German-born American physicist (1879–1955)

It is better to suffer wrong than to do it, and happier to be sometimes cheated than not to trust.

Samuel Johnson, British author and lexicographer (1709–1784)

Every man must get to Heaven his own way.

Frederick II ("the Great"), king of Prussia (1712–1786)

YOU CAN WIN BY FRAUD AND DECEIT,
BUT EVIL LEAVES AN ITCH YOU CAN'T SCRATCH

Forgive, son; men are men; they needs must err.

Euripides, Greek dramatist (480?–406 B.C.)

Wickedness is always easier than virtue, for it takes the short cut to everything.

James Boswell, Scottish biographer (1740–1795)

He who commits injustice is ever made more wretched than he who suffers it.

Plato, Greek philosopher (427?–347 B.C.)

Let justice be done though the heavens fall.

Roman maxim

I expect to pass through life but once. If, therefore, there be any kindness I can show or any good thing I can do to any fellow being, let me do it now and not defer or neglect it, as I shall not pass this way again.

William Penn, English Quaker colonizer in America (1644–1718)

YOU CAN WIN BY FRAUD AND DECEIT,
BUT EVIL LEAVES AN ITCH YOU CAN'T SCRATCH

He that is without sin among you, let him cast the first stone.

Jesus of Nazareth

What is morality in any given time or place? It is what a majority then and there happen to like, and immorality is what they dislike.

Alfred North Whitehead, British philosopher
(1861–1947)

My own experience and development deepen every day my conviction that our moral progress may be measured by the degree in which we sympathize with individual suffering and individual joy.

George Eliot (Mary Ann Evans), British novelist
(1819–1880)

The confidence in another man's virtue is no light evidence of a man's own, and God willingly favors such a confidence.

Michel Eyquem de Montaigne, French essayist
(1533–1592)

YOU CAN WIN BY FRAUD AND DECEIT,
BUT EVIL LEAVES AN ITCH YOU CAN'T SCRATCH

It is almost impossible systematically to constitute a natural moral law. Nature has no principles. She furnishes us with no reason to believe that human life is to be respected. Nature, in her indifference, makes no difference between right and wrong.

Anatole France, French author (1844–1924)

Of all the benefits which virtue confers on us, the contempt of death is one of the greatest.

Michel Eyquem de Montaigne, French essayist (1533–1592)

I shall never permit myself to stoop so low as to hate any man.

Booker T. Washington, American educator and author (1856–1915)

The action is best that secures the greatest happiness for the greatest number.

Francis Hutcheson, Irish-born Scottish philosopher (1694–1746)

YOU CAN WIN BY FRAUD AND DECEIT,
BUT EVIL LEAVES AN ITCH YOU CAN'T SCRATCH

And now abideth faith, hope, and charity, these three, but the greatest of these is charity.

The First Letter of Paul to the Corinthians

And what is the greatest number? Number one.

David Hume, Scottish philosopher and historian (1711–1776)

No man is above the law, and no man is below it; nor do we ask any man's permission when we require him to obey it.

Theodore Roosevelt, U.S. president (1858–1919)

Forgiveness is the scent that the rose leaves on the heel that crushes it.

Anonymous

First secure an independent income, then practice virtue.

Greek proverb

YOU CAN WIN BY FRAUD AND DECEIT,
BUT EVIL LEAVES AN ITCH YOU CAN'T SCRATCH

Here is a rule to remember in the future, when anything tempts you to be bitter: not, "This is a misfortune" but "To bear this worthily is good fortune."

Marcus Aurelius, Roman emperor and philosopher (121–180)

One ought to examine himself for a very long time before thinking of condemning others.

Molière (Jean Baptiste Poquelin), French dramatist (1622–1673)

See in what peace a Christian can die.

Joseph Addison, English essayist (1672–1719), to his son on his deathbed

 To spend life for something which outlasts it.

William James, American psychologist and philosopher (1842–1910)

Imagine Where We'd Be If We Didn't Possess Our Glorious Curiosity

Oh how fine it is to know a thing or two!

Molière (Jean Baptiste Poquelin), French dramatist (1622–1673)

Knowledge itself is power.

Francis Bacon, English statesman, philosopher, and essayist (1561–1626)

I attribute the little I know to my not having been ashamed to ask for information, and to my . . . conversing with all descriptions of men on those topics that form their own peculiar professions and pursuits.

John Locke, English philosopher (1632–1704)

I am defeated, and know it, if I meet any human being from whom I find myself unable to learn anything.

George Herbert Palmer, American educator (1842–1933)

IMAGINE WHERE WE'D BE
IF WE DIDN'T POSSESS OUR GLORIOUS CURIOSITY

To generalize is to be an idiot. To particularize is alone the distinction of merit—general knowledges are those knowledges that idiots possess.

William Blake, British poet (1757–1827)

The important thing is not to stop questioning. Curiosity has its own reasoning for existing. . . . Never lose a holy curiosity.

Albert Einstein, German-born American physicist (1877–1955)

The degree of one's emotion varies inversely with one's knowledge of the facts—the less you know the hotter you get.

Bertrand Russell, British philosopher (1872–1970)

And even in our sleep pain that cannot forget falls drop by drop upon the heart, and in our own despair, against our will, comes wisdom to us by the awful grace of God.

Aeschylus, Greek dramatist (526–456 B.C.)

IMAGINE WHERE WE'D BE
IF WE DIDN'T POSSESS OUR GLORIOUS CURIOSITY

Aristotle could have avoided the mistake of thinking that women have fewer teeth than men by the simple device of asking Mrs. Aristotle to open her mouth.

Bertrand Russell, British philosopher (1872–1970)

In 1583 Galileo Galilei . . . a youth of nineteen attending prayers in the baptistery of the Cathedral of Pisa, was, according to tradition, distracted by the swinging of the altar lamp. No matter how wide the swing of the lamp, it seemed that the time it took the lamp to move from one end to the other was the same. Of course Galileo had no watch, but he checked the intervals of the swing by his own pulse. This curious everyday puzzle, he said, enticed him away from the study of medicine to which his father had committed him to the study of mathematics and physics. He had discovered . . . that the time of a pendulum's swing varies not with the width of the swing but with the length of the pendulum.

Daniel J. Boorstin, American historian (1914—)

IMAGINE WHERE WE'D BE
IF WE DIDN'T POSSESS OUR GLORIOUS CURIOSITY

The hunger and thirst for knowledge, the keen delight in the chase, the good humored willingness to admit that the scent was false, the eager desire to get on with the work, the cheerful resolution to go back and begin again, the broad good sense, the unaffected modesty, the imperturbable temper, the gratitude for any little help that was given—all these will remain in my memory though I cannot paint them for others.

Frederic William Maitland, British jurist and historian (1850–1906)

I went to the woods because I wished to live deliberately, to front only the essential facts of life, and see if I could not learn what it had to teach, and not, when I came to die, discover that I had not lived. I did not wish to live what was not life. . . . I wanted to live so sturdily and so Spartan-like as to put to rout all that was not life . . . to drive life into a corner . . . to know it by experience and be able to give an account of it in my next excursion.

Henry David Thoreau, American philosopher (1817–1862)

IMAGINE WHERE WE'D BE
IF WE DIDN'T POSSESS OUR GLORIOUS CURIOSITY

The growth of wisdom may be gauged exactly by the diminution of ill-temper.

Friedrich Wilhelm Nietzsche, German philosopher.
(1844–1900)

Wisdom does not show itself so much in precept as in life—in a firmness of mind and mastery of appetite. It teaches us to do as well as talk; and to make our actions and words all of a color.

Lucius Annaeus Seneca, Roman author
(4 B.C.–A.D. 65)

The most manifest sign of wisdom is a continual cheerfulness; her state is like that in the regions above the moon, always clear and serene.

Michel Eyquem de Montaigne, French essayist
(1533–1592)

I tell you the past is a bucket of ashes.

Carl Sandburg, American poet (1878–1967)

IMAGINE WHERE WE'D BE
IF WE DIDN'T POSSESS OUR GLORIOUS CURIOSITY

Men on their side must force themselves for a while to lay their notions by and begin to familiarize themselves with facts.

Francis Bacon, English statesman, philosopher, and essayist (1561–1626)

Curiosity . . . endows the people who have it with a generosity in argument and a serenity in their own mode of life which springs from their cheerful willingness to let life take the form it will.

Alistair Cooke, British-born American broadcaster and author (1908—)

The mind never need stop growing. Indeed, one of the few experiences which never pall is the experience of watching one's own mind and how it produces new interests, responds to new stimuli, and develops new thoughts, apparently without effort and almost independently of one's own conscious control.

Gilbert Highet, Scottish-born American classicist (1906–1978)

IMAGINE WHERE WE'D BE
IF WE DIDN'T POSSESS OUR GLORIOUS CURIOSITY

There is much pleasure to be gained from useless knowledge.

Bertrand Russell, British philosopher (1872–1970)

What can I know? What ought I to do? What can I hope?

Immanuel Kant, German philosopher (1724–1804)

A woman especially, if she have the misfortune of knowing any thing, should conceal it as well as she can.

Jane Austen, British author (1775–1817)

IMAGINE WHERE WE'D BE
IF WE DIDN'T POSSESS OUR GLORIOUS CURIOSITY

The Minute He Opened His Mouth You Could Tell He Read Books

A man who does not read good books has no advantage over the man who can't read them.

Mark Twain (Samuel L. Clemens), American humorist (1835–1910)

To sit alone in the lamplight with a book spread out before you and hold intimate converse with men of unseen generations—such is pleasure beyond compare.

Yoshido Kenko, Japanese Buddhist priest and poet (b. 1283)

When I get a little money, I buy books; and if any is left, I buy food and clothes.

Desiderius Erasmus, Dutch humanist and theologian (1524–1583)

I've never known any trouble that an hour's reading didn't assuage.

Charles de Secondat, Baron de Montesquieu, French political philosopher (1689–1755)

THE MINUTE HE OPENED HIS MOUTH
YOU COULD TELL HE READ BOOKS

A room without books is a body without a soul.

Marcus Tullius Cicero, Roman statesman and orator (106–43 B.C.)

Books are the legacies that a great genius leaves to mankind, which are delivered down from generation to generation as presents to the posterity of those who are yet unborn.

Joseph Addison, English essayist (1672–1719)

The reading of all good books is like a conversation with all the finest men of past centuries.

René Descartes, French mathematician and philosopher (1596–1650)

Then I thought of reading—the nice and subtle happiness of reading . . . this joy not dulled by age, this polite and unpunishable vice, this selfish, serene, lifelong intoxication.

Logan Pearsall Smith, American essayist (1865–1946)

THE MINUTE HE OPENED HIS MOUTH
YOU COULD TELL HE READ BOOKS

Without books the development of civilization would have been impossible. They are the engines of change, windows on the world, "lighthouses" as the poet said "erected in the sea of time." They are companions, teachers, magicians, bankers of the treasures of the mind. Books are humanity in print.

Barbara Tuchman, American historian (1912–1989)

To put away one's own original thoughts in order to take up a book is a sin against the Holy Ghost.

Arthur Schopenhauer, German philosopher (1788–1860)

My early and invincible love of reading I would not exchange for all the riches of India.

Edward Gibbon, British historian (1737–1794)

A good book is the precious lifeblood of a master spirit embalmed and treasured up on purpose to a life beyond life.

John Milton, English poet (1608–1674)

THE MINUTE HE OPENED HIS MOUTH
YOU COULD TELL HE READ BOOKS

When I am attacked by gloomy thoughts, nothing helps me so much as running to my books. They quickly absorb me and banish the clouds from my mind.

Michel Eyquem de Montaigne, French essayist (1533–1592)

The World of Books
Is the Most Remarkable Creation of Man.
Nothing Else That He Builds Ever Lasts.
Monuments Fall;
Nations Perish;
Civilizations Grow Old and Die Out;
And After an Era of Darkness,
New Races Build Others.
But in the World of Books Are Volumes
That Have Seen This Happen Again and Again
And Yet Live On.
Still Young,
Still As Fresh As the Day They Were Written,
Still Telling Men's Hearts,
Of the Hearts of Men Centuries Dead.

Clarence Day, American author (1874–1935)

THE MINUTE HE OPENED HIS MOUTH
YOU COULD TELL HE READ BOOKS

I cannot live without books.

Thomas Jefferson, U.S. president (1743–1826)

People say life is the thing, but I prefer reading.

Logan Pearsall Smith, American essayist (1865–1946)

Taste is only to be educated by contemplation, not of the tolerably good but of the truly excellent. I therefore show you only the best works; and when you are grounded in these, you will have a standard for the rest, which you will know how to value, without overrating them.

Johann Wolfgang von Goethe, German author (1749–1832)

THE MINUTE HE OPENED HIS MOUTH
YOU COULD TELL HE READ BOOKS

If You
Take Your Time,
Thinking
Is Fun

I thought about it all the time.

Sir Isaac Newton, English scientist (1642–1727), on how he discovered the law of gravity

The gods plant reason in mankind, of all good gifts the highest.

Sophocles, Greek dramatist (496?–406 B.C.)

When he thinks about something, he doesn't think about it a little bit, he thinks about it with all his heart and soul.

A colleague's description of Dr. Harold Urey (1893–1981), nuclear physicist and lunar geologist

Desire to know why, and how—curiosity, which is a lust of the mind, that a perseverance of delight in the continued and indefatigable generation of knowledge—exceedeth the short vehemence of any carnal pleasure.

Thomas Hobbes, English philosopher (1588–1679)

IF YOU TAKE YOUR TIME, THINKING IS FUN

Mental fight means thinking against the current, not with it. . . . It is our business to puncture gas bags and discover the seeds of truth.

Virginia Woolf, British author (1882–1941)

Men give me credit for some genius. All the genius I have is this: When I have a subject in mind, I study it profoundly. Day and night it is before me. My mind becomes pervaded with it . . . the effort which I have made is what people are pleased to call the fruit of genius. It is the fruit of labor and thought.

Alexander Hamilton, American statesman (1755?–1804)

There seemed to be one quality of mind which seemed to be of special and extreme advantage in leading him to make discoveries. It was the power of never letting exceptions go unnoticed.

Francis Darwin, on his father, Charles Darwin, British naturalist (1809–1882)

IF YOU TAKE YOUR TIME, THINKING IS FUN

Thought is great and swift and free, the light of the world, the chief glory of man.

Bertrand Russell, British philosopher (1872–1970)

The great tragedy of science—the slaying of a beautiful hypothesis by an ugly fact.

Thomas Henry Huxley, British zoologist (1825–1895)

 If I have made any valuable discoveries, it has been owing more to patient attention than to any other talent.

Sir Isaac Newton, English scientist (1642–1727)

The fundamental fact about the Greek was that he had to use his mind. The ancient priests had said, "Thus far and no farther. We set the limits of thought." The Greek said, "All things are to be examined and called into question. There are no limits set on thought."

Edith Hamilton, German-born American classicist (1867–1963)

IF YOU TAKE YOUR TIME, THINKING IS FUN

For I say unto you in all sadness of conviction that to think great thoughts you must be heroes as well as idealists. Only when you have worked alone—when you have felt around you a black gulf of solitude more isolating than that which surrounds the dying man, and in hope and despair have trusted to your own unshaken will—then only can you gain the secret isolated joy of the thinker, who knows that a hundred years after he is dead and forgotten men who have never heard of him will be moving to the measure of his thought—the subtle rapture of postponed power, which the world knows not because it has no external trappings, but which to his prophetic vision is more real than that which commands an army. And if this joy should not be yours, still it is only thus you can know that you have done what lay in you to do—can say that you have lived, and be ready for the end.

Oliver Wendell Holmes, Jr., American jurist
(1841–1935)

Genius is eternal patience.

Michelangelo Buonarroti, Italian artist (1475–1564)

IF YOU TAKE YOUR TIME, THINKING IS FUN

A sedentary life is the real sin against the Holy Spirit. Only those thoughts that come by walking have any value.

Friedrich Wilhelm Nietzsche, German philosopher (1844–1900)

Thought is subversive and revolutionary, destructive and terrible; thought is merciless to privilege, established institutions, and comfortable habit.

Bertrand Russell, British philosopher (1872–1970)

Action and faith enslave thought, both of them in order not to be troubled or inconvenienced by reflection, criticism, and doubt.

General Henri Frederic Amiel, Swiss educator and philosopher (1821–1881)

The temptation to form premature theories upon insufficient data is the bane of our profession.

Sherlock Holmes, fictional character by Sir Arthur Conan Doyle, British author (1859–1930)

IF YOU TAKE YOUR TIME, THINKING IS FUN

Most of the things we do, we do for no better reason than that our fathers have done them or our neighbors do them, and the same is true of a larger part than what we suspect of what we think.

Oliver Wendell Holmes, Jr., Amerian jurist (1841–1935)

Men are apt to mistake the strength of their feeling for the strength of their argument. The heated mind resents the chill touch and relentless scrutiny of logic.

William Ewart Gladstone, British political leader (1809–1898)

The beginning of wisdom is a definition of terms.

Socrates, Greek philosopher (470?–399 B.C.)

Every great advance in natural knowledge has involved the absolute rejection of authority.

Thomas Henry Huxley, British zoologist (1825–1895)

IF YOU TAKE YOUR TIME, THINKING IS FUN

The minute a phrase becomes current, it becomes an apology for not thinking accurately to the end of the sentence.

Oliver Wendell Holmes, Jr., American jurist (1841–1935)

Many a man fails to become a great thinker only because his memory is too good.

Friedrich Wilhelm Nietzsche, German philosopher (1844–1900)

If any man wishes to write a clear style, let him first be clear in his thoughts.

Johann Wolfgang von Goethe, German author (1749–1832)

 I lived in solitude in the country and noticed how the monotony of a quiet life stimulates the creative mind.

Albert Einstein, German-born American physicist (1877–1955)

IF YOU TAKE YOUR TIME, THINKING IS FUN

Man is not logical, and his intellectual history is a record of mental reserves and compromises. He hangs on to what he can find of his old beliefs even when he is compelled to surrender their logical basis.

John Dewey, American philosopher and educator (1859–1952)

Familiar things happen, and mankind does not bother about them. It requires a very unusual mind to undertake the analysis of the obvious.

Alfred North Whitehead, British philosopher (1861–1947)

'Tis the mind that makes the body rich.

William Shakespeare, English dramatist (1564–1616)

I thought so hard I got a headache.

J. D. Cobb, student, on why his paper was late

IF YOU TAKE YOUR TIME, THINKING IS FUN

To find the exact answer, one must first ask the exact question.

S. Tobin Webster, British Anglican clergyman
(1896–1962)

No statement should be believed because it is made by an authority.

Hans Reichenbach, German-born American
philosopher and educator (1891–1953)

I am not a disbeliever in those who have told me they went to bed in the evening with an unsolved problem on their mind and woke up in the morning to find, waiting for them there in their consciousness, the correct answer.

Dr. Jean Hanson, British biophysicist and zoologist
(1919–1973)

Good Health Brings You Lots Of Vigor; And, Boy, Does That Make You Tired!

A sound mind in a sound body is a short but full description of a happy state in this world.

John Locke, English philosopher (1632–1704)

Give me health and a day, and I will make the pomp of emperors ridiculous.

Ralph Waldo Emerson, American author (1803–1882)

Cheerfulness is the best promoter of health and is as friendly to the mind as to the body.

Joseph Addison, English essayist (1672–1719)

I am convinced digestion is the great secret of life.

Rev. Sydney Smith, British clergyman and author (1771–1845)

A merry heart doeth good like a medicine.

The Book of Proverbs

GOOD HEALTH BRINGS YOU LOTS OF VIGOR;
AND, BOY, DOES THAT MAKE YOU TIRED!

Avoid fresh meats which angry up the blood. If your stomach disputes you, lie down and pacify it with cool thoughts. Keep the juices flowing by jangling around gently as you move. Go very light in the vices such as carrying on in society. The social ramble ain't restful. Don't look back. Someone might be gaining on you.

Leroy (Satchel) Paige, American baseball player (1906–1982), on staying young

True enjoyment comes from activity of the mind and exercise of the body: the two are ever united.

Baron Alexander von Humboldt, German naturalist, author, and statesman (1769–1859)

Too much attention to health is a hindrance to learning, to invention, and to studies of any kind, for we are always feeling suspicious shootings and swimmings in our heads, and we are prone to blame studies for them.

Plato, Greek philosopher (427?–347 B.C.)

GOOD HEALTH BRINGS YOU LOTS OF VIGOR;
AND, BOY, DOES THAT MAKE YOU TIRED!

Why do strong arms fatigue themselves with frivolous dumbbells? To dig a vineyard is worthier exercise for men.

Martial (Marcus Valerius Martialis), Roman epigrammatist (c. 40–104)

Look to your health; and if you have it, praise God and value it next to conscience; for health is the second blessing that we mortals are capable of, a blessing money cannot buy.

Izaak Walton, English angler and author (1593–1683)

It is the sign of a dull mind to dwell upon the cares of the body, to prolong exercise, eating and drinking, and other bodily functions. These things are best done by the way; all your attention must be given to the mind.

Epictetus, Greek Stoic philosopher (c. 50–120)

 Natural forces within us are the true healers of disease.

Hippocrates, Greek physician (460?–377? B.C.)

GOOD HEALTH BRINGS YOU LOTS OF VIGOR;
AND, BOY, DOES THAT MAKE YOU TIRED!

To be free minded and cheerfully disposed at hours of meat and sleep and of exercise is one of the best precepts of long lasting.

Francis Bacon, English statesman, philosopher, and essayist (1561–1626)

What can be added to the happiness of a man who is in health, out of debt, and has a clear conscience?

Adam Smith, Scottish political economist and philosopher (1723–1790)

If you be sick, your own thoughts make you sick.

Ben Jonson, English dramatist (1573–1637)

Refuse to be ill. Never tell people you are ill; never own it to yourself. Illness is one of those things which a man should resist on principle at the outset.

Edward Bulwer-Lytton, Baron Lytton, British author (1803–1873)

GOOD HEALTH BRINGS YOU LOTS OF VIGOR; AND, BOY, DOES THAT MAKE YOU TIRED!

How do you live a long life?
"Take a two-mile walk every morning before
breakfast."

*Harry S. Truman, U.S. president (1884–1972), on
his eightieth birthday*

It is impossible to walk rapidly and be unhappy.

*Dr. Howard Murphy, American physician
(1856–1920)*

How a sickness enlarges the dimensions of a
man's self to himself! He is his own exclusive
object. Supreme selfishness is inculcated in him
as his only duty.

Charles Lamb, British essayist (1775–1834)

Walking is man's best medicine.

Hippocrates, Greek physician (460?–377? B.C.)

I consider being ill as one of the great pleasures
of life, provided one is not too ill.

Samuel Butler, British novelist (1835–1902)

GOOD HEALTH BRINGS YOU LOTS OF VIGOR;
AND, BOY, DOES THAT MAKE YOU TIRED!

Good Talkers Go A Long Way —Learn To Talk

The reason why so few people are agreeable in conversation is that each is thinking more about what he intends to say than what others are saying.

François, Duc de La Rochefoucauld, French author (1613–1680)

Good nature is more agreeable in conversation than wit and gives a certain air to the countenance which is more amiable than beauty.

Joseph Addison, English essayist (1672–1719)

Conversation has a kind of charm about it, an insinuating and insidious something that elicits secrets just like love or liquor.

Lucius Annaeus Seneca, Roman author (4 B.C.–A.D. 65)

Speech is civilization itself. The word . . . preserves contact—it is silence which isolates.

Thomas Mann, German-born American author (1875–1955)

In my opinion, the most fruitful and natural play of the mind is in conversation. I find it sweeter than any other action in life; and if I were forced to choose, I think I would rather lose my sight than my hearing and voice. The study of books is a drowsy and feeble exercise which does not warm you up.

Michel Eyquem de Montaigne, French essayist
(1533–1592)

Conversation. What is it? A mystery! It's the art of never seeming bored, of touching everything with interest, of pleasing with trifles, of being fascinating with nothing at all. How do we define this lively darting about with words, of hitting them back and forth, this sort of brief smile of ideas which should be conversation?

Guy de Maupassant, French author (1850–1893)

The happiest conversation is that of which nothing is distinctly remembered but a general effect of pleasing impression.

Samuel Johnson, British author and lexicographer
(1709–1784)

Never speak of yourself to others; make them talk about themselves instead; therein lies the whole art of pleasing. Everybody knows it, and everyone forgets it.

Edmond and Jules de Goncourt, French authors (1822–1896; 1830–1870)

We are growing serious, and let me tell you, that's the next step to being dull.

Joseph Addison, English essayist (1672–1719)

Listening well and answering well is one of the greatest perfections that can be obtained in conversation.

François, Duc de La Rochefoucauld, French author (1613–1680)

Conversation would be vastly improved by the constant use of four simple words: I do not know.

André Maurois, French author (1885–1967)

There is one topic peremptorily forbidden to all well-bred, to all rational mortals, namely, their distempers. If you have not slept, or if you have slept, or if you have a headache, or sciatica, or leprosy, or thunderstoke, I beseech you, by all the angels, to hold your peace and not pollute the morning.

Ralph Waldo Emerson, American author (1803–1882)

If you can't say anything good about someone, sit right here next to me.

Alice Roosevelt Longworth, American socialite and wit (1884–1980)

Confidence is courage at ease.

Daniel Maher, American psychologist (1941—)

Every man becomes, to a certain degree, what the people he generally converses with are.

Philip Dormer Stanhope, Earl of Chesterfield, English statesman and author (1694–1773)

Gossip and shop talk! That's the fun of a job.

Young woman on lunch break overheard in Baltimore café

A Good Laugh Is Sunshine In The House

Blessed is he who makes his companions laugh.

The Koran

The most wasted of all days is that on which one has not laughed.

Sébastien-Roche Nicolas Chamfort, French author (1741–1794)

There is a form [of laughter] that springs from the heart, heard every day in the merry voice of childhood, the expression of a laughter-loving spirit that defies analysis by the philosopher, which has nothing rigid or mechanical in it, and totally without social significance. Bubbling spontaneously from the heart of child or man, without egotism and full of feeling, laughter is the music of life.

Sir William Osler, Canadian-born British physician (1849–1919)

A good laugh is sunshine in the house.

William Makepeace Thackeray, British author (1811–1863)

I am sure that since I have had the full use of my reason, nobody has heard me laugh.

Philip Dormer Stanhope, Earl of Chesterfield, English statesman and author (1694–1773)

No man who has once heartily and wholly laughed can be altogether irreclaimably bad.

Thomas Carlyle, Scottish historian (1795–1881)

The two best physicians of them all—Dr. Laughter and Dr. Sleep.

Gregory Dean, Jr., British physician (1907–1979)

Sudden glory is the passion which makes those grimaces called laughter.

Thomas Hobbes, English philosopher (1588–1679)

I quickly laugh at everything for fear of having to cry.

Pierre Augustin Caron de Beaumarchais, French author (1732–1799)

If you like a man's laugh before you know anything of him, you may say with confidence that he is a good man.

Feodor Dostoyevsky, Russian author (1821–1881)

Laughter is the cipher key wherewith we decipher the whole man.

Thomas Carlyle, Scottish historian (1795–1881)

Laughter does not seem to be a sin, but it leads to sin.

Saint John Chrysostom, Antioch-born Greek church father (345?–407)

Let
Us Swear
Eternal
Friendship

Have friends. 'Tis a second existence.

Baltasar Gracián, Spanish philosopher (1601–1658)

I look upon every day to be lost in which I do not make a new acquaintance.

Samuel Johnson, British author and lexicographer (1709–1784)

The mind is so rarely disturbed, but that the company of a friend will restore it to some degree of tranquility and sedateness.

Adam Smith, Scottish political economist (1723–1790)

When friendship disappears then there is a space left open to that awful loneliness of the outside world which is like the cold space between the planets. It is an air in which men perish utterly.

Hilaire Belloc, French-born British author (1870–1953)

LET US SWEAR ETERNAL FRIENDSHIP

Who does not in some sort live to others, does not live much to himself.

Michel Eyquem de Montaigne, French essayist (1533–1592)

Friendship is almost always the union of a part of one mind with part of another; people are friends in spots.

George Santayana, Spanish-born American educator and philosopher (1863–1952)

Have no friends not equal to yourself.

Confucius, Chinese philosopher (551–479 B.C.)

Do not choose for your friends and familiar acquaintances those that are of an estate or quality too much above yours. . . . You will hereby accustom yourselves to live after their rate in clothes, in habit, and in expenses, whereby you will learn a fashion and rank of life above your degree and estate, which will in the end be your undoing.

Matthew Hale, English jurist (1609–1676)

The men and women who make the best boon companions seem to have given up hope of doing something else . . . some defect of talent or opportunity has cut them off from their pet ambition and has thus left them with leisure to take an interest in the lives of others. Your ambitious man is selfish. No matter how secret his ambition may be, it makes him keep his thoughts at home. But the heartbroken people—if I may use the word in a mild, benevolent sense—the people whose wills are subdued to fate, give us consolation, recognition, and welcome.

John Chapman (Johnny Appleseed), American author (1775?–1845)

I desire to so conduct the affairs of this administration that if at the end, when I come to lay down the reins of power, I have lost every other friend on earth, I shall at least have one friend left, and that friend shall be down inside of me.

Abraham Lincoln, U.S. president (1809–1865)

LET US SWEAR ETERNAL FRIENDSHIP

So long as we love we serve; so long as we are loved by others, I would almost say we are indispensable; and no man is useless while he has a friend.

Robert Louis Stevenson, Scottish author (1850–1894)

If a man does not make new acquaintances as he advances through life, he will soon find himself alone. A man, Sir, should keep his friendship in constant repair.

Samuel Johnson, British author and lexicographer (1709–1784)

Madam, I have been looking for a person who dislikes gravy all my life: let us swear eternal friendship.

Rev. Sydney Smith, British clergyman and essayist (1771–1845)

Business, you know, may bring you money, but friendship hardly ever does.

Jane Austen, British author (1775–1817)

Consult your friend on all things, especially on those which respect yourself. His counsel may then be useful where your own self-love might impair your judgement.

Lucius Annaeus Seneca, Roman author
(4 B.C.–A.D. 65)

Living With Nature— Those Were The Good Times!

God almighty first planted a garden; and, indeed, it is the purest of human pleasures.

Francis Bacon, English statesman, philosopher, and essayist (1561–1626)

Call for the grandest of all earthly spectacles, what is that? It is the sun going to his rest.

Thomas De Quincey, British essayist (1785–1859)

Today I have grown taller from walking with the trees.

Karl Baker, Australian naturalist (1865–1951)

A cloudy day or a little sunshine have as great an influence on many constitutions as the most recent blessings or misfortunes.

Joseph Addison, English essayist (1672–1719)

When chill November's surly blast
Make fields and forest bare.

Robert Burns, Scottish poet (1759–1796)

LIVING WITH NATURE—THOSE WERE THE GOOD TIMES!

Nothing is worth more than this day.

Johann Wolfgang von Goethe, German author
(1749–1832)

For many years I was a self-appointed inspector of snowstorms and rainstorms and did my duty faithfully, though I never received payment for it.

Henry David Thoreau, American philosopher
(1817–1862)

For what human ill does dawn not seem to be an alternative?

Thornton Wilder, American author (1897–1975)

For the man sound of body and serene of mind there is no such thing as bad weather; every day has its beauty, and storms which whip the blood do but make it pulse more vigorously.

George Robert Gissing, British novelist and critic
(1857–1903)

LIVING WITH NATURE—THOSE WERE THE GOOD TIMES!

I must go down to the seas again, to the lonely
  sea and sky,
And all I ask is a tall ship and a star to steer
  her by.

John Masefield, British poet (1878–1967)

For, lo, the winter is past, the rain is over and
gone; the flowers appear on the earth; the time
of the singing of birds is come, and the voice of
the turtle is heard in our land.

Song of Solomon

The flower in the vase smiles, but no longer
laughs.

Malcom De Chazal, French writer (1902–1981)

There is a pleasure in the pathless woods,
There is a rapture on the lonely shore,
There is society, where none intrudes,
By the deep sea, and music in it roars:
I love not man the less, but Nature more.

*George Gordon, Lord Byron, British poet
(1788–1824)*

LIVING WITH NATURE—THOSE WERE THE GOOD TIMES!

One could do worse than be a swinger of birches.

Robert Frost, American poet (1874–1963)

Summer afternoon—summer afternoon; to me those have always been the two most beautiful words in the English language.

Henry James, American novelist and critic (1843–1916)

I love the rain. I want the feeling of it on my face.

Katherine Mansfield, New Zealand-born British author (1888–1923)

The first fall of snow is not only an event, it is a magical event. You go to bed in one kind of a world and wake up in another quite different, and if this is not enchantment then where is it to be found?

John Boynton (J. B.) Priestly, British author (1894–1984)

LIVING WITH NATURE—THOSE WERE THE GOOD TIMES!

Summer is delicious, rain is refreshing, wind braces up, snow is exhilarating; there is no such thing as bad weather, only different kinds of good weather.

John Ruskin, British author and critic (1819–1900)

If winds are the spirit of the sky's ocean, the clouds are its texture. Theirs is easily the most uninhibited dominion of the earth. Nothing in physical shape is too fantastic for them. They can be round as apples or as fine as string, as dense as a jungle, as wispy as a whiff of down, as mild as puddle water or as potent as the belch of a volcano. Some are thunderous anvils formed by violent updrafts from the warm earth. Some are ragged coattails of storms that have passed. Some are stagnant blankets of warm air resting on cold. . . . I have seen clouds in the dawn that looked like a pink Sultan with his pale harem maidens and a yellow slob of eunuch lolling impotent in the background.

Guy Murchie, American author (1907—)

The sky is the daily bread of the eyes.

Ralph Waldo Emerson, American author
(1803–1882)

Now is the season for sailing; for already the chattering swallow is come and the pleasant west wind; the meadows bloom and the sea, tossed up with waves and rough blasts, has sunk to silence. Weigh thine anchors and unloose thy hawsers, O Mariner, and sail with all thy canvas set.

Leonidas of Tarentum, Greek poet
(c. 290–c. 220 B.C.)

May the countryside and the gliding valley streams content me. Lost to fame, let me love river and woodland.

Virgil (Publius Vergilius Maro), Roman poet
(70–19 B.C.)

Roll on, thou deep and dark blue ocean, roll!

George Gordon, Lord Byron, British poet
(1788–1824)

LIVING WITH NATURE—THOSE WERE THE GOOD TIMES!

THE BOOK OF SUCCESS

The most serious charge that can be brought against New England is not Puritanism but February.

Joseph Wood Krutch, American educator and naturalist (1893–1970)

There is not, in my opinion, anything more mysterious in nature than the instinct of animals, which thus rise above reason, and yet fall infinitely short of it.

Joseph Addison, English essayist (1672–1719)

St. Agnes' Eve—Ah, bitter chill it was!
The owl, for all his feathers, was a-cold.
The hare limped trembling through the frozen
    grass,
And silent was the flock in wooly fold.

John Keats, British poet (1795–1821)

To create a little flower is the labor of ages.

William Blake, British poet (1757–1827)

LIVING WITH NATURE—THOSE WERE THE GOOD TIMES!

If you want to be happy for a year, plant a garden; if you want to be happy for life, plant a tree.

English proverb

The melancholy days are come, the saddest of
the year,
Of wailing winds, and naked woods and
meadows brown and sear.

William Cullen Bryant, American poet (1794–1878)

See one promontory, one mountain, one sea, one river and see all.

Socrates, Greek philosopher (470?–399 B.C.)

The planting of trees is the least self-centered of all that we can do. It is a purer act of faith than the procreation of children.

Thornton Wilder, American author (1897–1975)

The sea—this truth must be confessed—has no generosity. No display of manly qualities—courage, hardihood, endurance, faithfulness—has ever been known to touch its irresponsible consciousness of power.

Joseph Conrad, Polish-born British author (1857–1924)

Nature in her indifference makes no distinction between good and evil.

Anatole France, French author (1844–1924)

The forest is the poor man's overcoat.

Maine proverb

Only those within whose own consciousness the suns rise and set, the leaves burgeon and wither, can be said to be aware of what living is.

Joseph Wood Krutch, American educator and naturalist (1893–1970)

LIVING WITH NATURE—THOSE WERE THE GOOD TIMES!

Honest winter, snow clad and with the frosted beard, I can welcome not uncordially; but that long deferment of the calendar's promise, that weeping loom of March and April, that bitter blast outraging the honour of May—how often has it robbed me of heart and hope.

George Robert Gissing, British novelist and critic (1857–1903)

April comes like an idiot, babbling and strewing flowers.

Edna St. Vincent Millay, American poet (1892–1950)

Scenery is fine, but human nature is finer.

John Keats, British poet (1795–1821)

To sit in the shade on a fine day and look upon verdure is the most perfect refreshment.

Jane Austen, British author (1775–1817)

LIVING WITH NATURE—THOSE WERE THE GOOD TIMES!

Oh the wild joys of living! The leaping from rock to rock . . . the cool silver shock of the plunge in a pool's living waters.

Robert Browning, British poet (1812–1889)

What a book a devil's chaplain might write on the clumsy, wasteful, blundering, low, and horribly cruel work of nature!

Charles Darwin, British naturalist (1809–1882)

Nature's laws affirm instead of prohibit. If you violate her laws, you are your own prosecuting attorney, judge, jury, and hangman.

Luther Burbank, American horticulturist (1849–1926)

The seasons . . . are what a symphony ought to be: four perfect movements in harmony with each other.

Arthur Rubenstein, Polish-born American pianist (1887–1982)

LIVING WITH NATURE—THOSE WERE THE GOOD TIMES!

The roaring of the wind is my wife, and the stars through the window pane are my children.

John Keats, British poet (1795–1821)

I want death to find me planting my cabbages.

Michel Eyquem de Montaigne, French essayist (1533–1592)

Autumn arrives in early morning, but Spring at the close of a winter day.

Elizabeth Bowen, Irish-born British author (1899–1973)

In those vernal seasons of the year, when the air is calm and pleasant, it were an injury and sullenness against Nature not to go out and see her riches and partake in her rejoicing with heaven and earth.

John Milton, English poet (1608–1674)

LIVING WITH NATURE—THOSE WERE THE GOOD TIMES!

He that plants trees loves others besides himself.

British proverb

Thank heaven, the sun has gone in, and I don't have to go out and enjoy it.

Logan Pearsall Smith, American essayist
(1865–1946)

18

Happiness
Is A
By-Product

Happiness is a by-product.

Robert Trany, American writer (1928—)

Many who seem to be struggling with adversity are happy; many, amid great affluence, are utterly miserable.

Publius Cornelius Tacitus, Roman historian and orator (55?–120?)

To live happily is an inward power of the soul.

Marcus Aurelius, Roman emperor and philosopher (121–180)

As far as the job of President goes, it's rewarding and I've given before this group the definition of happiness for the Greeks. I'll define it again: the full use of your powers along lines of excellence. I find, therefore, that the Presidency provides some happiness.

John F. Kennedy, U.S. president (1917–1963)

The mind is master over every kind of fortune; itself acts in both ways, being the cause of its own happiness and misery.

Lucius Annaeus Seneca, Roman author
(4 B.C.–A.D. 65)

As happy a man as any in the world, for the whole world seems to smile upon me!

Samuel Pepys, English diarist (1633–1703)

Human felicity is produced not as much by great pieces of good fortune that seldom happen as by little advantages that occur every day.

Benjamin Franklin, American statesman and author
(1706–1790)

The secret of happiness is this: let your interests be as wide as possible, and let your reactions to the things and persons that interest you be as far as possible friendly rather than hostile.

Bertrand Russell, British philosopher (1872–1970)

HAPPINESS IS A BY-PRODUCT

Happiness is not best achieved by those who seek it directly.

Bertrand Russell, British philosopher (1872–1970)

The happiness or unhappiness of men depends as much on their humours as on fortune.

François, Duc de La Rochefoucauld, French author (1613–1680)

The goal towards which the pleasure principle impels us—of becoming happy—is not attainable; yet we may not—nay, cannot—give up the effort to come nearer to realization of it by some means or other.

Sigmund Freud, Austrian psychiatrist (1856–1939)

We are long before we are convinced that happiness is never to be found; and each believes it possessed by others, to keep alive the hope of obtaining it for himself.

Samuel Johnson, British author and lexicographer (1709–1784)

HAPPINESS IS A BY-PRODUCT

There is only one way to happiness, and that is to cease worrying about things which are beyond the power of our will.

Epictetus, Greek Stoic philosopher (c. 50–120)

Happiness is the only sanction of life; when happiness fails, existence remains a mad and lamentable experience.

George Santayana, Spanish-born American educator and philosopher (1863–1952)

My hopes are not always realized, but I always hope.

Ovid (Publius Ovidius Naso), Roman poet (43 B.C.–A.D. 18)

If you are distressed by anything external, the pain is not due to the thing itself, but to your estimate of it; and thus you have the power to revoke it at any minute.

Marcus Aurelius, Roman emperor and philosopher (121–180)

My happiness derives from knowing the people I love are happy.

Holly Ketchel, contemporary American writer

Formula of my happiness: a Yes, a No, a straight line, a goal.

Friedrich Wilhelm Nietzsche, German philosopher (1844–1900)

Hope is itself a species of happiness, and perhaps the chief happiness which this world affords.

Samuel Johnson, British author and lexicographer (1709–1784)

To be happy in this world, especially when youth is past, it is necessary to feel oneself not merely an isolated individual whose day will soon be over, but part of the stream of life slowing on from the first germ to the remote and unknown future.

Bertrand Russell, British philosopher (1872–1970)

HAPPINESS IS A BY-PRODUCT

We French found it and called it *joie de vivre*—
the joy of living.

Renée Repond, French actress (1888–1965)

Wellbeing is attained by little and little, and
nevertheless is no little thing itself.

Zeno, Greek philosopher (335–263 B.C.)

How to gain, how to keep, how to recover
happiness is in fact for most men at all times the
secret motive of all they do, and of all they are
willing to endure.

*William James, American psychologist and
philosopher (1842–1910)*

The happiest people are those who seem to
have no particular reason for being happy except
that they are so.

*William Ralph Inge, British prelate and theologian
(1860–1964)*

HAPPINESS IS A BY-PRODUCT

We must interpret a bad temper as a sign of inferiority.

Alfred Adler, Austrian psychiatrist (1870–1937)

Power tends to corrupt, and absolute power corrupts absolutely.

John Emrich Dalberg-Acton, Lord Acton, British historian (1834–1902)

And I Thought I Was The Only Person Who Had An Inferiority Complex

The mind is its own place, and in itself
Can make heav'n of hell, a hell of heav'n.

John Milton, English poet (1608–1674)

Men's activities are occupied in two ways—in grappling with external circumstances and in striving to set things at one in their own topsy-turvy mind.

William James, American psychologist and philosopher (1842–1910)

A man's first care should be to avoid the reproaches of his own heart, and his next to escape the censures of the world.

Joseph Addison, English essayist (1672–1719)

Look into the depths of your own soul and learn first to know yourself, then you will understand why this illness was bound to come upon you and perhaps you will thenceforth avoid falling ill.

Sigmund Freud, Austrian psychiatrist (1856–1939)

AND I THOUGHT I WAS THE ONLY PERSON
WHO HAD AN INFERIORITY COMPLEX

The perfectly normal person is rare in our civilization.

Karen Horney, German-born American psychoanalyst (1885–1952)

All sins have their origin in a sense of inferiority otherwise called ambition.

Cesare Pavese, Italian poet (1908–1950)

He took over anger to intimidate subordinates, and in time anger took over him.

Saint Albertus Magnus, German religious philosopher (1206?–1280)

Of all the infirmities we have, the most savage is to despise our being.

Michel Eyquem de Montaigne, French essayist (1533–1592)

To be human means to feel inferior.

Alfred Adler, Austrian psychiatrist (1870–1937)

AND I THOUGHT I WAS THE ONLY PERSON
WHO HAD AN INFERIORITY COMPLEX

Life for both sexes is arduous, difficult, a perpetual struggle. . . . More than anything . . . it calls for confidence in oneself. . . . And how can we generate this imponderable quality most quickly? By thinking that other people are inferior to oneself.

Virginia Woolf, British author (1882–1941)

We have long observed that every neurosis has the result, and therefore probably the purpose, of forcing the patient out of real life, of alienating him from actuality.

Sigmund Freud, Austrian psychiatrist (1856–1939)

He [Freud] often said three things were impossible to fulfill completely: healing, education, governing. He limited his goals in analytic treatment to bringing the patient to the point where he could work for a living and learn to love.

Theodore Reik, American psychoanalyst (1888–1969)

AND I THOUGHT I WAS THE ONLY PERSON
WHO HAD AN INFERIORITY COMPLEX

Rancor is an outpouring of a feeling of inferiority.

José Ortega y Gasset, Spanish philosopher, author, and politician (1883–1955)

The feeling of inferiority rules the mental life and can be clearly recognized in the sense of incompleteness and unfulfillment, and in the uninterrupted struggle both of individuals and humanity.

Alfred Adler, Austrian psychiatrist (1870–1931)

The more sinful and guilty a person tends to feel, the less chance there is that he will be a happy, healthy, or law-abiding citizen. . . . He will become a compulsive wrong-doer.

Dr. Albert Ellis, American psychologist (1913—)

Where love rules, there is no will to power; where power predominates, there love is lacking. The one is the shadow of the other.

Carl Gustav Jung, Swiss psychiatrist (1875–1961)

AND I THOUGHT I WAS THE ONLY PERSON
WHO HAD AN INFERIORITY COMPLEX

Neurotics complain of their illness, but they make the most of it, and when it comes to taking it away from them they will defend it like a lioness her young.

Sigmund Freud, Austrian psychiatrist (1856–1939)

The "sensitiveness" claimed by neurotics is matched by their egotism: they cannot abide the flaunting by others of the sufferings to which they pay an ever increasing amount of attention in themselves.

Marcel Proust, French author (1871–1922)

The test of one's behavior pattern: relationship to society, relationship to one's work, relationship to sex.

Alfred Adler, Austrian psychiatrist (1870–1937)

No passion so effectively robs the mind of its powers of acting and reasoning as fear.

Edmund Burke, British politician and orator (1729–1797)

AND I THOUGHT I WAS THE ONLY PERSON
WHO HAD AN INFERIORITY COMPLEX

A day spent without the sight or sound of beauty, the contemplation of mystery, or the search of truth or perfection is a poverty-stricken day; and a succession of such days is fatal to human life.

Lewis Mumford, American author and critic (1895–1990)

There are few human emotions as warm, comforting, and enveloping as self-pity. And nothing is more corrosive and destructive. There is only one answer: turn away from it and move on.

Dr. Megan Reik, contemporary American counselor

There's one blessing only, the source and cornerstone of beatitude—confidence in self.

Lucius Annaeus Seneca, Roman author (4 B.C.–A.D. 65)

Show me a sane man, and I will cure him for you.

Carl Gustav Jung, Swiss psychiatrist (1875–1961)

AND I THOUGHT I WAS THE ONLY PERSON
WHO HAD AN INFERIORITY COMPLEX

Anger is short madness.

Horace (Quintus Horatius Flaccus), Roman poet (65–8 B.C.)

Everything great that we know has come from neurotics. . . . Never will the world be aware of how much it owes to them, nor above all what they have suffered in order to bestow their gifts on it.

Marcel Proust, French author (1871–1922)

We are all prone to the malady of the introvert who, with the manifold spectacle of the world spread out before him, turns away and gazes only upon the emptiness within. But let us not imagine there is anything grand about the introvert's unhappiness.

Bertrand Russell, British philosopher (1872–1970)

The girl who can't dance says the band can't play.

Yiddish proverb

AND I THOUGHT I WAS THE ONLY PERSON
WHO HAD AN INFERIORITY COMPLEX

The

Facts

Of Life

A man can be himself only so long as he is alone.

Arthur Schopenhauer, German philosopher
(1788–1860)

A desire to be observed, considered, esteemed, praised, beloved, and admired by his fellows is one of the earliest as well as the keenest dispositions discovered in the heart of man.

John Adams, U.S. president (1735–1826)

Look, when that crowd gets to cheering, when we know they're with us, when we know they like us, we play better. A hell of a lot better!

Bill Carlin, American professional football player

I never come back home with the same moral character I went out with; something or other becomes unsettled where I had achieved internal peace; some one or other of the things I had put to flight reappears on the scene.

Lucius Annaeus Seneca, Roman author
(4 B.C.–A.D. 65)

If one of us could ascend to the heavenly realm and for a few hours accompany the divine on His daily rounds, he would see below millions of his fellow humans busily hurling themselves into the passions, sports, and action of the moment—all the while seemingly oblivious of those around him. But if our observer had the power and omniscience of the Lord, he would also feel and sense, pulsing through and vibrating from every one of us here below, a desperate and unending plea, "Notice me! I want to be known, admired, and loved by the whole world!" And it is this, this glorious weakness, this dependence of ours on each other, that makes some of us heroes and some of us fools—and most of us usually heroes and fools at the same time.

Rev. Michael Burry, British Anglican theologian
(1860–1938)

How much trouble he avoids who does not look to see what his neighbor says or does or thinks.

Marcus Aurelius, Roman emperor and philosopher
(121–180)

THE FACTS OF LIFE

The achievements which society rewards are won at the cost of dimunition of personality.

Carl Gustav Jung, Swiss psychiatrist (1875–1961)

When we talk in company we lose our unique tone of voice, and this leads us to make statements which in no way correspond to our real thoughts.

Friedrich Wilhelm Nietzsche, German philosopher (1844–1900)

Public opinion is a permeating influence, and it exacts obedience to itself; it requires us to think other men's thoughts, to speak other men's words, to follow other men's habits.

Walter Bagehot, British social scientist (1826–1877)

I care not so much what I am in the opinion of others, as what I am in my own; I would be rich of myself and not by borrowing.

Michel Eyquem de Montaigne, French essayist (1533–1592)

Character is formed in the stormy billows of the world.

> Johann Wolfgang von Goethe, German author (1749–1832)

No man lives without jostling and being jostled; in all ways he has to elbow himself through the world, giving and receiving offense.

> Thomas Carlyle, Scottish historian (1795–1881)

We become actors without realizing it, and actors without wanting to.

> General Henri Frédéric Amiel, Swiss educator and philosopher (1821–1881)

Live unknown.

> Epicurus, Greek philosopher (342–270 B.C.)

I am willing to love all mankind except an American.

> Samuel Johnson, British author and lexicographer (1709–1784)

You don't learn to hold your own in the world by standing on guard, but by attacking and getting well hammered yourself.

George Bernard Shaw, Irish-born British playwright (1856–1950)

The crowd gives the leader new strength.

Evenius, Roman scholar (42 B.C.–A.D. 13)

We live thick and are in each other's way, and stumble over one another, and I think we thus lose some respect for one another.

Henry David Thoreau, American philosopher (1817–1862)

I hate a fellow whom pride, or cowardice, or laziness drives into a corner, and who does nothing when he is there but sit and growl; let him come out as I do, and bark.

Samuel Johnson, British author and lexicographer (1709–1784)

To act from pure benevolence is not possible for finite human beings. Human benevolence is mingled with vanity, interest, or some other motive.

Samuel Johnson, British author and lexicographer
(1709–1784)

For what do we live but to make sport for our neighbors, and laugh at them in turn?

Jane Austen, British author (1775–1817)

The command to love our neighbors as ourselves . . . is impossible to fulfill.

Sigmund Freud, Austrian psychiatrist (1856–1939)

Fame always brings loneliness. Success is as ice cold and lonely as the North Pole.

Vicky Baum, Austrian-born American author
(1896–1960)

It is the nature of ambition to make men liars and cheaters, to hide the truth in their breasts, and show, like jugglers, another thing in their mouths, to cut all friendships and enmities to the measure of their own interests, and to make good countenance without the help of good will.

Sallust (Gaius Sallustius Crispus), Roman historian (86–34 B.C.)

It's The Niceties That Make The Difference

Fate gives us the hand, and we play the cards.

Arthur Schopenhauer, German philosopher
(1788–1860)

Remember this, that very little is needed to make a happy life.

Marcus Aurelius, Roman emperor and philosopher
(121–180)

Possessions, outward success, publicity, luxury—to me these have always been contemptible. I assume that a simple and unassuming manner of life is best for everyone, best for both the body and the mind.

Albert Einstein, German-born American physicist
(1879–1955)

I hold this as a rule of life: Too much of anything is bad.

Terence (Publius Terentius Afer), Roman author
(190?–59 B.C.)

The great and glorious masterpiece of man is to live to the point. All other things—to reign, to hoard, to build—are at most but inconsiderable props and appendages. The truly wise man must be as intelligent and expert in the use of natural pleasures as in all other functions of life. So the sages live, gently yielding to the laws of our human lot, to Venus and to Bacchus. Relaxation and versatility, it seems to me, go best with a strong and noble mind, and do it singular honor. There is nothing more notable in Socrates than that he found time, when he was an old man, to learn music and dancing, and thought them time well spent.

Michel Eyquem de Montaigne, French essayist (1533–1592)

The main things which seem to me important on their own account, and not merely as a means to other things, are knowledge, art, instinctive happiness, and relations of friendship or affection.

Bertrand Russell, British philosopher (1872–1970)

IT'S THE NICETIES THAT MAKE THE DIFFERENCE

The aim of life is some way of living, as flexible and gentle as human nature; so that ambition may stoop to kindness, and philosophy to candor and humor. Neither prosperity nor empire nor heaven can be worth winning at the price of a virulent temper, bloody hands, an anguished spirit, and a vain hatred of the rest of the world.

George Santayana, Spanish-born American educator and philosopher (1863–1952)

The impression forces itself upon one that men measure by false standards, that everyone seeks power, success, riches for himself, and admires others who attain them, while undervaluing the truly precious things in life.

Sigmund Freud, Austrian psychiatrist (1856–1939)

Look up, laugh loud, talk big, keep the colour in your cheek and the fire in your eye, adorn your person, maintain your health, your beauty and your animal spirits.

William Hazlitt, British essayist (1778–1830)

IT'S THE NICETIES THAT MAKE THE DIFFERENCE

To live lightheartedly but not recklessly; to be gay without being boisterous; to be courageous without being bold; to show trust and cheerful resignation without fatalism—this is the art of living.

Jean de La Fontaine, French fabulist (1621–1695)

The root of the matter . . . the thing I mean . . . is love, Christian love, or compassion. If you feel this, you have a motive for existence, a guide for action, a reason for courage, an imperative necessity for intellectual honesty.

Bertrand Russell, British philosopher (1872–1970)

Change your thoughts, and you change your world.

Norman Vincent Peale, American clergyman and author (1898—)

The shoe that fits one person pinches another; there is no recipe for living that suits all cases.

Carl Gustav Jung, Swiss psychiatrist (1875–1961)

IT'S THE NICETIES THAT MAKE THE DIFFERENCE

One ought, every day at least, to hear a little song, read a good poem, see a fine picture, and, if it were possible, to speak a few reasonable words.

Johann Wolfgang von Goethe, German author
(1749–1832)

This is what you shall do: love the earth, and sun, and animals, despise riches, give alms to every one that asks, stand up for the stupid and crazy, devote your income and labor to others, hate tyrants, argue not concerning God, have patience and indulgence toward the people, take off your hat to nothing known or unknown, or to any man or number of men; go freely with powerful uneducated persons, and with the young, and mothers of families; read these leaves in the open air every season of every year of your life; re-examine all you have been told at school or church, or in any books, and dismiss whatever insults your own soul.

Walter (Walt) Whitman, American poet
(1819–1892)

My heart, which is so full to overflowing, has often been solaced and refreshed by music when sick and weary.

Martin Luther, German Protestant religious reformer (1483–1546)

Music and woman I cannot but give way to, whatever my business is.

Samuel Pepys, English diarist (1633–1703)

We should consider every day lost in which we have not danced at least once.

Friedrich Wilhelm Nietzsche, German philosopher (1844–1900)

Beauty of style and harmony and grace and good rhythm depend on simplicity.

Plato, Greek philosopher (427?–347 B.C.)

Exuberance is beauty.

William Blake, British poet (1757–1827)

Music, the greatest good that mortals know,
And all of heaven we have below.

Joseph Addison, English essayist (1672–1719)

Without music, life would be an error. The German imagines even God singing songs.

Friedrich Wilhelm Nietzsche, German philosopher (1844–1900)

The moment we indulge our affections, the earth is metamorphosed; here is no winter and no night; all tragedies, all ennuis vanish—all duties even.

Ralph Waldo Emerson, American author (1803–1882)

Life is an end in itself, and the only question as to whether it is worth living is whether you have enough of it.

Oliver Wendell Holmes, Jr., American jurist (1841–1935)

He has achieved success who has lived well, laughed often, and loved much.

Bessie Stanley, contemporary American counselor

Few people have ever seriously wished to be exclusively rational. The good life which most desire is a life warmed by passions and touched with that ceremonial grace which is impossible without some affectionate loyalty to traditional forms and ceremonies.

Joseph Wood Krutch, American educator and naturalist (1893–1970)

Make no little plans; they have no magic to stir men's blood, and probably themselves will not be realized.

Daniel Hudson Burnham, American architect (1846–1912)

He that is discontented in one place will seldom be content in another.

Aesop, Greek fabulist (c. 550 B.C.)

We deem those happy who from the experience of life have learned to bear its ills without being overcome by them.

Carl Gustav Jung, Swiss psychiatrist (1875–1961)

He who has a why to live can bear almost any how.

Friedrich Wilhelm Nietzsche, German philosopher (1844–1900)

How does it happen, Maecenas, that no one is content with that lot which he has chosen or which chance has thrown his way, but praises those who follow a different course?

Horace (Quintus Horatius Flaccus), Roman poet (65–8 B.C.)

Indolence is a delightful but distressing state; we must be doing something to be happy. Action is no less necessary than thought to the instinctive tendencies of the human frame.

Mohandas Karamchand (Mahatma) Gandhi, Indian political leader (1869–1948)

Civilization . . . is a matter of imponderables, of delight in the things of the mind, of love of beauty, of honor, grace, courtesy, delicate feeling. Where imponderables are things of first importance, there is the height of civilization, and, if at the same time, the power of art exists unimpaired, human life has reached a level seldom attained and very seldom surpassed.

Edith Hamilton, German-born American classicist (1867–1963)

In everything, satiety closely follows the greatest pleasures.

Marcus Tullius Cicero, Roman statesman and orator (106–43 B.C.)

I like to walk about among the beautiful things that adorn the world; but private wealth I should decline, or any sort of personal possessions, because they would take away my liberty.

George Santayana, Spanish-born American educator and philosopher (1863–1952)

We never reflect how pleasant it is to ask for nothing.

Lucius Annaeus Seneca, Roman author
(4 B.C.–A.D. 65)

One word frees us of all the weight and pain of life. That word is love.

Sophocles, Greek dramatist (496?–406 B.C.)

Has a woman who knew she was well-dressed ever caught a cold?

Friedrich Wilhelm Nietzsche, German philosopher
(1844–1900)

At the touch of love, everyone becomes a poet.

Plato, Greek philosopher (427?–347 B.C.)

The ultimate of being successful is the luxury of giving yourself the time to do what you want to do.

Leontyne Price, American opera soprano (1927—)

In this world there are only two tragedies. One is not getting what one wants, and the other is getting it.

Oscar Wilde, Irish-born British author (1854–1900)

Do not spoil what you have by desiring what you have not; but remember that what you now have was once among the things you only hoped for.

Epicurus, Greek philosopher (342–270 B.C.)

I have no pleasure in any man who despises music. It is no invention of ours: it is a gift of God. I place it next to theology. Satan hates music: he knows how it drives the evil spirit out of us.

Martin Luther, German Protestant religious reformer (1483–1546)

Alas, after a certain age, every man is responsible for his own face.

Albert Camus, French author (1913–1960)

IT'S THE NICETIES THAT MAKE THE DIFFERENCE

There is no course of life so weak and sottish as that which is ordered by orders, method, and discipline.

Michel Eyquem de Montaigne, French essayist (1533–1592)

You have your way. I have my way. As for the right way, the correct way, and the only way, it does not exist.

Friedrich Wilhelm Nietzsche, German philosopher (1844–1900)

What a wonderful life I've had! I only wish I'd realized it sooner!

Colette (Sidonie Gabrielle Colette), French novelist (1873–1954)

What is the use of running when we are on the wrong road?

Bavarian proverb

Home: My Spot On Earth —The Place Where I Belong

The family is nature's masterpiece.

George Santayana, Spanish-born American educator and philosopher (1863–1952)

Do not choose your wife at the dance, but in a field of grain among the harvesters.

Slavic proverb

It was so cold the other day, I almost got married.

Shelley Winters, American actress (1922—)

There is nothing so much seduces reason from vigilance as the thought of passing life with an amiable woman in marriage.

Samuel Johnson, British author and lexicographer (1709–1784)

I married beneath me—all women do.

Nancy, Lady Astor, American-born British politician (1879–1964)

Such a wife as I want . . . must be young, handsome (I lay most stress upon a good shape), sensible (a little learning will do), well-bred, chaste, and tender. As to religion, a moderate stock will satisfy me. She must believe in God and hate a saint.

Alexander Hamilton, American statesman (1755?–1804)

There certainly are not so many men of large fortune in the world as there are of pretty women to deserve them.

Jane Austen, British author (1775–1817)

When two people are under the influence of the most violent, most insane, most elusive, and most transient of passions, they are required to swear that they will remain in that excited, abnormal, and exhausting condition continuously till death do them part.

George Bernard Shaw, Irish-born British playwright (1856–1950)

HOME: MY SPOT ON EARTH—THE PLACE WHERE I BELONG

There is no more lovely, friendly, and charming relationship, communion, or company than a good marriage.

Martin Luther, German Protestant religious reformer (1483–1546)

It happens as one sees in cages: the birds who are outside despair of ever getting in, and those within are equally desirous of getting out.

Michel Eyquem de Montaigne, French essayist (1533–1592)

The happiest moments of my life have been the few I have passed at home in the bosom of my family.

Thomas Jefferson, U.S. president (1743–1826)

Any intelligent woman, who reads the marriage contract and then goes into it, deserves all the consequences.

Isadora Duncan, American dancer (1878–1927)

Marriage has many pains, but celibacy has no pleasures.

Samuel Johnson, British author (1709–1784)

In nine cases out of ten, a woman had better show more affection than she feels.

Jane Austen, British author (1775–1817)

Better be quarreling than lonesome.

Irish proverb

The difference is wide that the sheets will not decide.

English proverb

When widows exclaim loudly against second marriages, I would always lay a wager that the man, if not the wedding day, is absolutely fixed on.

Henry Fielding, British author (1707–1754)

HOME: MY SPOT ON EARTH—THE PLACE WHERE I BELONG

A baby is God's opinion that life should go on.

Carl Sandburg, American author (1878–1967)

God couldn't be everywhere, so he created mothers.

Jewish proverb

Kissing don't last; cookery do!

George Meredith, British author (1828–1909)

My home. . . . It is my retreat and resting place from the wars. I try to keep this corner as a haven against the tempest outside, as I do another corner in my soul.

Michel Eyquem de Montaigne, French essayist (1533–1592)

Heaven will be no heaven to me if I do not meet my wife there.

Andrew Jackson, U.S. president (1767–1845)

As much as I converse with sages and heroes, they have very little of my love and admiration. I long for rural and domestic scenes, for the warbling of birds and the prattling of my children.

John Adams, U.S. president (1735–1826)

Alimony is like buying oats for a dead horse.

Arthur (Bugs) Baer, American journalist (1886–1969)

'Tis strange what a man may do, and a woman yet think him an angel.

William Makepeace Thackeray, British author (1811–1863)

There is in every woman's heart a spark of heavenly fire which lies dormant in the broad daylight of prosperity, but which kindles up and beams and blazes in the dark hour of adversity.

Washington Irving, American author (1783–1859)

HOME: MY SPOT ON EARTH—THE PLACE WHERE I BELONG

I believe love produces a certain flowering of the whole personality which nothing else can achieve.

Ivan Sergeevich Turgenev, Russian novelist
(1818–1883)

If I loved you Wednesday,
What is that to you?
I do not love you Thursday—
So much is true.

Edna St. Vincent Millay, American poet
(1892–1950)

These impossible women! How they do get around us! The poet was right: Can't live with them, or without them.

Aristophanes, Greek dramatist (488?–380? B.C.)

CHAPTER

23

A
Reminder

This also—that I live, I consider a gift of God.

Ovid (Publius Ovidius Naso), Roman poet
(43 B.C.–A.D. 18)

Death twitches my ear. "Live," he says, "I am coming."

Virgil (Publius Vergilius Maro), Roman poet
(70–19 B.C.)

Our lives as we lead them are passed on to others, whether in physical or mental forms, tingeing all future lives together. This should be enough for one who lives for truth and service to his fellow passengers on the way.

Luther Burbank, American horticulturist
(1849–1926)

The short bloom of our brief and narrow life flies fast away. While we are calling for flowers and wine and women, old age is upon us.

Juvenal (Decimus Junius Juvenalis), Roman satirist
(60?–140?)

A REMINDER

Our dead brothers still live for us and bid us think of life, not death—of life to which in their youth they lent the passion and glory of Spring. As I listen, the great chorus of life and joy begins again, and amid the awful orchestra of seen and unseen powers and destinies of good and evil, our trumpets sound once more a note of daring, hope, and will.

Oliver Wendell Holmes, Jr., American jurist (1841–1935), Memorial Day address 1884

I came to the place of my birth and cried, "The friends of my youth, where are they?" And echo answered, "Where are they?"

Arab proverb

Like Confucius of old, I am so absorbed in the wonder of the earth and the life upon it, that I cannot think of heaven and the angels.

Pearl S. Buck, American author (1892–1973)

A REMINDER

If there is a sin against life, it consists . . . in hoping for another life and in eluding the implacable grandeur of this life.

Albert Camus, French author (1913–1960)

Warm summer sun,
shine kindly here.
Warm southern wind,
blow softly here.
Green sod above,
lie light, lie light.
Good night, dear heart,
Good night, good night.

Mark Twain (Samuel L. Clemens), American humorist (1835–1910), epitaph for his daughter

On the whole, I am on the side of the unregenerate who affirms the worth of life as an end in itself, as against the saints who deny it.

Oliver Wendell Holmes, Jr., American jurist (1841–1935)

A REMINDER

In the final act of the play, Our Town, *Emily, a young mother, has died and gone to Heaven. In the following scene, she has received permission to go back to earth for one day where, alone and unseen by the earthlings, she can once again be with her family and friends. The experience unnerves her. The dialogue comes at the end of her brief stay on earth.*

Emily:
I can't. I can't go on. It goes so fast. We don't have time to look at one another. (She breaks down sobbing.) I didn't realize. So all that was going on and we never noticed. Take me back—up the hill—to my grave. But first, wait! One more look.

Good-by; good-by, world; good-by, Grover's Corners . . . Mama and Papa. Good-by to clocks ticking . . . and Mama's sunflowers. And food and coffee. And new-ironed dresses and hot baths . . . and sleeping and waking up. Oh, earth, you're too wonderful for anybody to realize you. (She looks toward the stage manager and asks abruptly through her tears.) Do any human beings ever realize life while they live it?—every, every minute?

A REMINDER

Stage Manager:
No. (Pause) The saints and poets, maybe—they do some.

Emily:
I'm ready to go back.

Thornton Wilder, American playwright (1897–1975), Our Town